Assessing Learning:
Quality Standards and
Institutional Commitments

Third Edition

Donna Younger, EdD
Catherine Marienau, PhD

CAEL
Linking Learning and Work

The Council for Adult & Experiential Learning
Chicago

Kendall Hunt
p u b l i s h i n g   c o m p a n y

For David O. Justice

With deepest appreciation for his many contributions
to advance the field of Adult Learning

 CAEL

The Council for Adult & Experiential Learning
55 East Monroe Street, Suite 1930
Chicago, Illinois 60603
www.cael.org

Manufactured in the United States of America
10 9 8 7 6 5 4 3 2

CONTENTS

Foreword vii

Chapter 1. *Introduction to Assessing Learning*. *1*

The Growing Role for Assessment in Higher Education. 2

Assessment's Role with PLA and CBE 4

Key Institutional Commitments for Assessing Learning. 6

Chapter Preview 7

References. 8

Chapter 2. *Foundational Perspectives on Learning*
from Experience*. *13

Goal #1: Assessment Processes Can Be Designed to
Elicit Genuine Learning 14

Goal #2: Assessment Processes Can Be Designed to
Foster New Learning. 15

Goal #3: Assessment Processes Can Be Designed to Engage
Learners' Critical Reflection on Their Experience 16

References. 18

Chapter 3. *Quality Standards for Assessing Learning:*
A Commitment to Inquiring and Deliberating about
Assessment in Context* *21

Quality Standards for Assessing Learning 22

I. Credit or competencies are awarded only for evidence
of learning, not for experience or time spent. 22

II. Assessment is integral to learning because it leads to
and enables future learning. 23

III. Assessment is based on criteria for outcomes that are
clearly articulated and shared among constituencies. . . . 24

IV. The determination of credit awards and competency
levels are made by appropriate subject matter and
credentialing experts. 25

V. *Assessment advances the broader purpose of access and equity for diverse individuals and groups to support their success.* 26

VI. *Institutions proactively provide guidance and support for learners' full engagement in the assessment process.* . 27

VII. *Assessment policies and procedures are the result of inclusive deliberation and are shared with all constituencies.* 28

VIII. *Fees charged for assessment are based on the services performed in the process rather than the credit awarded..* 29

IX. *All practitioners involved in the assessment process pursue and receive adequate training and continuing professional development for the functions they perform.* 30

X. *Assessment programs are regularly monitored, evaluated, and revised to respond to institutional and learner needs.* 31

Standards and Questions to Guide Deliberations & Decisions. 32

Shifts in Quality Standards. 35

References. 39

Chapter 4. *Aligning Practices with Purposes: A Commitment to Aligning Assessment Practices with Institutional Purposes.* **41**

Institutional Purpose 1: The Development of Individuals . . . 43

Institutional Purpose 2: Serving Adults Intentionally. 50

Institutional Purpose 3: The Relevant Transfer of Learning from Education to Life. 54

Institutional Purpose 4: Ensuring Consistent Practice Across Institutions 58

Other Considerations for Practice 60

References. 61

Chapter 5. *Guiding Learning and Development in Assessment: A Commitment to the Evolving Expertise of Individuals and Institutions* *63*

    References. 71

Chapter 6. *Tools and Resources to Support PLA Implementation: A Commitment to Taking Action to Utilize Assessment Expertise* *73*

    Institutional Readiness Guide: Positioning Prior Learning Assessment 75

    Forming a PLA Leadership Group 83

    Initial Steps for the Leadership Group. 84

    Planning the Action Planning Process. 85

    PLA Policy template. 86

    Portfolio Development Models. 90

    References. 92

Chapter 7. *Misconceptions, Poor Practices, and Issues.* *93*

    Misconceptions 93

    Poor Practices 98

    Anticipated Issues 102

    In Conclusion 106

Appendix A. *Steps and Principles for Assessing Unsponsored Prior Experiential Learning* *107*

Appendix B. *Administrative Measures to Ensure Quality Principles and Procedures* *113*

Appendix C. *Writing Statements of Learning Outcomes* . . . *117*

Index *119*

FOREWORD

Those of us who spend our careers in higher education do so because we know how important it is to students and to society. In recent years, the rest of the world seems to have come on board as well. The reason they have done so is because our economy depends on—more than ever before—a skilled workforce. Today's jobs require workers with higher-order technical skills as well as strong critical thinking, communication, and problem-solving skills. More and more jobs are requiring some college education. Along with that, it has become clear that individual workers are also better off with more education; a college degree is what ensures that someone can earn a living wage and be more employable over a lifetime.

Along with the growing recognition of the importance of postsecondary credentials, we are seeing new delivery models, new educational providers, and new kinds of credentials such as badges. Yet, we are seeing skyrocketing tuition leading to questions from students and third party payers—like the federal government, state governments, and employers—about whether they are getting their money's worth. We hear reports of employers who are disappointed in the work readiness of new college graduates that they have hired.

All of these developments lead to a growing demand for an appropriate assessment of a student's learning. *How do we know* that students can learn through online and flexibly paced formats? *How do we know* that there is academic rigor in the programs offered through unaccredited vendors? *How do we know* if students are learning at all? These are all cries for evidence of learning, and high-quality assessment is the solution.

CAEL's interest in assessment predates these more recent trends. In the 1970s, higher education saw a growing number of adults enrolling in college, and new programs emerged to serve this new population. One important development within these programs was the interest in recognizing the value of learning rather than seat time. So colleges started to offer credit to students who had college-level learning that they had developed in their work and other life experiences, and colleges also developed competency-based degree programs that allowed students more flexible pathways to a degree, as long as they demonstrated their learning. Many faculty and administrators saw the logic in this—learning is learning. It should not matter how the learning was acquired. But there was great unease about how to make sure that the college-level learning was there. The solution, then as now, was high quality assessment.

CAEL has long held the belief that assessment can be more than just a tool for measuring learning. It is also a tool that, when done well, can help the learning process. Students who are given good feedback during the assessment process can use that feedback to build on what they know and turn it into new knowledge as well as a deeper understanding of themselves as learners. That's why we are sometimes accused of having a bit of a bias toward portfolio assessment: the act of developing a portfolio requires the student to reflect on their learning in an intentional way, not just after the assessment but also leading up to it.

Colleges rightly question how to do assessment of learning the right way, how to ensure that the process is academically sound, and how to do so in a way that makes assessment itself an important part of the educational journey. For the past 18 years, *Assessing Learning* has been answering those questions by providing standards for high-quality assessment of student learning. Back in 1989, the first edition of *Assessing Learning* was developed primarily for colleges engaged with prior learning assessment. The field was so new and faced resistance from the more traditional elements of the academy. The lack of accepted standards and practices meant that everyone was creating their own. CAEL provided training as one way to help, but the original Quality Standards for Assessing Learning codified the messages for those whom our training could not reach. It provided the necessary guardrails within which so many different and well-considered approaches to PLA could emerge and maneuver.

This third edition continues that tradition of providing standards and guidelines for the assessment of learning. As with the second edition in 2006, this version fine tunes some of the language to reflect contemporary concerns within higher education. It addition, it zooms out from a narrower focus on assessment for the award of credit for prior learning and acknowledges that these quality standards are important in other contexts as well—most notably, in programs designed around the assessment of competencies. Competency-based education (CBE) has been growing rapidly throughout higher education over the past five years, and the assessment of competencies is a critical component of these new programs that are designed to focus on what students know and can do rather than how many classes they took or credit hours they earned.

In this edition, the Quality Standards also recognizes the important role that assessment can play in advancing the broader purposes of equity and access in higher education. Assessment legitimizes the knowledge that is gained by people from diverse backgrounds and sets it on the same level as classroom-based learning. The college or university is not the sole authority of what knowledge and truth are. Students can construct knowledge and truth from their lived experience, and assessment can then help to make that learning a valued part of a formal higher education credential. This goes back to CAEL's own roots—our 1970s pedigree shows—and the view that alternative approaches to education are critical for advancing social justice and equal access.

Finally, the Quality Standards in this new edition of *Assessing Learning* advance the idea that assessment is more than just measuring learning. The standards boldly state that assessment *leads to and enables* future learning—that it should be seen by practitioners as an essential part of the learning process. And the new standards encourage institutions to provide students with guidance and support for learners' *full engagement in the assessment process*. It is only then that assessment can truly foster new learning and be more than just a tool or a way to check the box on a compliance requirement.

In this new era of higher education, it is exciting to see all of the new developments that are opening doors for adult learners. The focus on what students know and can do is a welcome part of these changes. We know that assessment can and should be a vital part of the learning process in these new contexts, and we are excited about how these new Quality Standards can advance ideas for how assessment can play an important role in fostering learning, expanding access, and providing innovative new models for the adult learner.

Pamela Tate
President and CEO, CAEL

INTRODUCTION TO ASSESSING LEARNING

Higher education is alive with the rebirth of assessment. Prior learning assessment (PLA), an innovation spawned over four decades ago by adult degree programs, is now being offered in some form in hundreds of colleges and universities. Assessment is an integral component of competency-based education (CBE), which is emerging across all levels and curricular areas, representing a wide variety of models. The assessment of student learning movement gained national attention in the early 1980s, notably in the report *Involvement in Learning* (National Institute of Education, 1984):

> *We thus believe assessment to be an organic part of learning. The use of tests to sort and screen is legitimate for professional certification and licensing and, indeed, for any operation where selection is necessary. But assessment has even greater potential as a tool for clarifying expectations and for increasing student involvement when it is used to measure improvements in performance. (p. 53)*

The view of assessment as an "organic part of learning" was notable at the time—but unfortunately short lived. George Kuh (in press) explains that multiple forces soon thereafter pulled assessment away from its "animating purpose... to improve student learning." Assessment for the purpose of

Institutional Commitments for Assessing Learning

1. A commitment to inquiring and deliberating about assessment in context.

2. A commitment to aligning assessment practices with institutional purposes.

3. commitment to the evolving expertise of individuals and institutions.

4. A commitment to taking action to utilize assessment expertise.

accountability became a primary driver, as higher education institutions sought to comply with requirements of regional accreditors, state agencies, and federal financial aid. In addition, the public at large has demanded more proof that investments in college are worth the time and money and that the outcomes include capacities for gainful employment, not just an inquisitive mind. Faced with multiple agendas, assessment within higher education has become more preoccupied with compliance rather than focused on learner achievement.

The Growing Role for Assessment in Higher Education

The good news, however, is that the current initiatives for assessment in general, in PLA, and in CBE are re-emphasizing assessment of student learning outcomes as well as the value of assessment to the student and to the degree granting enterprise. In addition, even beyond PLA and CBE, Kuh (in press) predicts that higher education is on the road to *"getting assessment back on the right track."* One example of this trend is a major 2016 initiative—the Excellence in Assessment (EIA) program—for institutions to assess student learning and use evidence of learning to improve teaching practices. Several national groups support this program: Voluntary System of Accountability (VSA), a joint initiative of the American Association of State Colleges and Universities (AASCU) and the Association of Public and Land-grant Universities (APLU), the Association of American Colleges and Universities (AAC&U),

and the National Institute of Learning Outcomes Assessment (NILOA). Through a rigorous review process, institutions compete for the EIA designation; those who receive the award serve as exemplars for taking assessment seriously and doing it effectively with regard to student performance, teaching effectiveness, and institutional accountability.

Further, national and local efforts to get assessment back on track can benefit from a strong and growing research base on student learning outcomes—in both general and professional education—that has covered the gamut of assessment, such as validity metrics, rubrics, and individual assessment methods themselves, including performance-based, project-based, self-assessment, prior learning, and portfolio evaluation. Long-standing leaders in research on learning outcomes assessment include Trudy Banta (1999; 2002), founder of *Assessment Update Journal* (since 1989) and convener of the Assessment Institute; Peter Ewell (2009) and his colleagues at NCHEMS (National Center for Higher Education Management Systems); Marcia Mentkowski and colleagues (2000) at Alverno College; and scholars associated with NILOA. The authors of *Using Evidence of Student Learning to Improve Higher Education* (Kuh, Ikenberry, Jankowski, Cain, Ewell, Hutchings, & Kinzie, 2015) make a compelling case for using evidence about student learning to improve teaching and learning. Their work also provides an informative historical review of the learning outcomes assessment movement.

Research specific to prior learning assessment and assessment in competency-based education is also growing. CAEL has expanded its research on prior learning assessment (Klein-Collins, 2012a, 2012b; Wilbur, Marienau, & Fiddler, 2012). In 2011, Travers and Mandell from SUNY Empire State College launched *Prior Learning Assessment Inside Out: An International Journal on Theory, Research and Practice in Prior Learning Assessment* (PLAIO). Contributing to the growth of scholarship on competency-based education, the *Journal of Competency-Based Education* was launched by Governors State University in 2016 (Johnstone, 2016). The new *Handbook of Research on Competency-based Education in University Settings* (Rasmussen, Northrup, & Colson, 2017) offers

website

a compendium of evidence-based approaches across higher education settings. Field-based inquiry has characterized the work of practitioners in the Competency-based Network (C-BEN), which has become "essentially the field's learning lab" (Council for Adult and Experiential Learning [CAEL], 2015, p. 3). Assessment of student learning has been one of C-BEN's priority areas for investigation. Using surveys and interviews, a working group cataloged assessment approaches and practices among CBE programs, which has informed a larger program design initiative.

The major trend in assessment of learning in higher education to move away from standardized tests and toward outcomes and rubrics will certainly stimulate even more research. Learning outcomes are criterion referenced; rubrics delineate criteria into more specific indicators for levels of achievement and usually contain a strategy for scoring, typically for grading and other evaluation purposes. National players are contributing frameworks for learning outcomes along with rubrics for assessment of learning within those frameworks. Lumina's Degree Qualifications Profile (DQP) (2014) articulates and distinguishes learning outcomes at associate, baccalaureate, and master's levels. For undergraduate education, AAC&U through its LEAP (Liberal Education for America's Promise) initiative, developed Essential Learning Outcomes (2007). AAC&U's well-accepted VALUE rubrics (Valid Assessment of Undergraduate Education) (Finley & Rhodes, 2013; Sullivan, 2015) are aligned with the proficiencies in the DQP. The DPQ and LEAP frameworks are "examples of how to *standardize the manner* in which authentic student learning can be measured without *standardizing* what, where, or how" (Kuh, in press).

Assessment's Role with PLA and CBE

PLA and CBE approaches are also examples of standardizing the "manner" of assessment but not the "what, where, or how." CBE and PLA both focus on the outcomes of learning as the primary referent in assessment while also regarding pathways for learning as more malleable. Practitioners seeking ways to offer greater flexibility to adult students are attracted to both PLA and CBE as educational interventions that permit—even invite—a range of learning experiences that lead to the same outcome. Given their shared vantage points, it is understandable that the two terms are often conflated.

However, CBE and PLA operationalize this shared philosophy differently. Competency-based education is an approach to developing academic programs that provides demonstrated outcomes as "an alternative to the credit-hour system of credentialing" (American Council on Education [ACE] & Blackboard, n.d., p. 4). A variety of models and strategies fall under the umbrella of CBE. However, all CBE programs focus on assuring that learners provide evidence of what they have learned and what they can do with it, even as they rely on different structures for dealing with the time and place of learning. Assessment strategies within CBE programs range from prescriptive assignments to more student-directed evidence of learning, but all are evaluated against clear statements of competence that call for demonstrated learning.

While CBE is an approach to program development, PLA represents a set of processes that enable learners to extract what they have learned from experience outside the academy and demonstrate that learning in ways that are credit worthy or competency worthy. PLA is a practice that may be employed within either CBE or conventional programs; it enacts its commitment to an outcomes-focus by ensuring that the outcomes of learning are assessed—rather than the means of learning. PLA relies on a variety of assessment methods and tools to provide an alternative pathway to credit or competence within a system. Whether it is designed to address course equivalencies or larger curriculum elements, such as program level outcomes, PLA may exist either within a CBE context or within a more traditional educational setting.

When PLA is used to demonstrate both what a student knows and is able to do, it is itself a type of competency-based approach to degree completion, and this is true whether students are matching their prior learning to a course-based program or a competency-based program. Students are required to prove and demonstrate, through assessment, what they know and can do. When integrated into traditional course based programs, PLA, therefore, brings a CBE component to those programs, allowing them to become partly competency based in the process.

PLA can therefore serve as a stepping stone from traditional non-CBE programs to CBE while supporting both traditional degrees and competency-based ones. (Tate & Klein-Collins, 2015). The consideration of the relationship between PLA and CBE will continue as both practices evolve and will inform the larger conversation about the variety of ways that outcomes-focused education manifests itself.

Key Institutional Commitments for Assessing Learning

Institutions that view assessment of student learning as a dynamic enterprise are poised to make and sustain **four key commitments**. First, they are committed to inquiring and deliberating about assessment in the context of their institution as well as the wider field. Second, they are committed to aligning assessment practices with institutional practices and purposes, which includes using data to drive program design and inform institutional effectiveness. Third, they are committed to building expertise of the institution and of all its stakeholders in assessment processes. Fourth, they are committed to taking action to bring assessment expertise to bear on various aspects of adult learning, including determining scale and starting points, targeting programs and populations, and using assessment data on student learning to influence institutional improvements.

Since 1989, *Assessing Learning* has provided guidance to institutions in how they design, administer, and manage the assessment of learning. The Standards for Assessing Learning described in the book provide important guardrails to ensure high-quality approaches to assessment while also allowing enough flexibility for institutions to use assessment in ways that best serve their students and their missions.

These institutional commitments call for effective strategies. Jack Lindquist's (1978)

FLOOR model of adaptive strategies for change fits with the emphasis of this third edition of *Assessing Learning* on making "institutional commitments" through dialogue and informed decision-making. The FLOOR model consists of Force, Linkage, Openness, Ownership, and Reward. External *forces*, such as accreditation and federal policies, along with leadership from the top (e.g., political heads of nation and state, presidents–provosts–deans in colleges and universities), are necessary for change but not sufficient. We also need to create stronger *linkages* within and across institutions as well as with our external partners (e.g., professional associations, workplaces). We need to exercise *openness* to new ideas and practices as well as to lessons from our own and others' experiences. We need to take *ownership* for creating and sustaining effective assessment practices that promote students' learning and academic success. We need to offer *rewards* that recognize the demanding responsibilities being shouldered by students, faculty, and administrators and we need to offer rewards that actually matter to the people involved.

Chapter Preview

This edition of *Assessing Learning* addresses assessment matters concerning adult and experiential learning from three key perspectives. First, in Chapter Two we examine assessment in relation to learning from experience through the lens of foundational theories. Second, in Chapter Three we provide an updated set of Standards, along with questions for deliberation, to help institutions generate policies and practices that complement their own context while observing national agreements. Third, recognizing the complexities involved in assessment of student learning, we offer the "framework of four commitments" to help institutions navigate what Rose and Leahy referred to as "not a static process but one of fundamental change and innovation" (1997, p. 97). After the discussion of the Standards, Chapter Three goes on to address the first institutional commitment: inquiring and deliberating about assessment in the context of the institution as well as the wider field. Chapter Four addresses the commitment to aligning assessment practices with institutional practices and purposes, which includes using data to drive program design and inform institutional effectiveness. Chapter Five addresses the commitment to building expertise of the institution and all of its stakeholders in assessment processes. Chapter Six addresses the commitment to taking action to bring assessment expertise to bear on various aspects of adult learning, including determining scale and starting points, targeting programs and populations, and using assessment data on student learning to influence institutional improvements. The seventh and final chapter reviews the hazards of malpractice in assessment and ways to adjust practice to avoid them.

We are fortunate to be able to draw on a rich theoretical base that can affirm and inform our practices in assessment of student learning. Recognizing CAEL's continuing commitment to adult learners, in the next chapter we highlight theories of adult learning and, in particular, theories about learning from experience.

References

American Council on Education & Blackboard. (n.d.) *Clarifying competency based education terms: A lexicon*. Washington, DC: Authors. Retrieved from http://bbbb.blackboard.com/Competency-based-education-definitions

Adelman, C., Ewell, P., Gaston, P., & Schneider, C. G. (2014). *The degree qualifications profile*. Indianapolis, IN: Lumina Foundation. Retrieved from https://www.luminafoundation.org/files/resources/dqp.pdf

Association of American Colleges & Universities. (2007). Washington, D.C. Author. Retrieved from https://www.aacu.org/sites/default/files/files/LEAP/GlobalCentury_final.pdf

Association of American Colleges & Universities. (2007). *VALUE rubrics*. Washington, DC: Author. Retrieved from https://www.aacu.org/value-rubrics

Banta, T. W. (Ed.). (launched in 1989). *Assessment update*. San Francisco, CA: John Wiley & Sons.

Banta, T. W., Jones, E. A., & Black, K. E. (2009). *Designing effective assessment: Principles and profiles of good practice.* San Francisco, CA: Jossey-Bass.

Council for Adult and Experiential Learning. (2015, June). *Competency-based education and quality assurance: Emerging themes discussed at the 2014 national convening.* Chicago, IL: Author. Retrieved from http://cdn2.hubspot.net/hubfs/617695/old_site_books/ 2014_CBE_Convening_Findings_Report.pdf

Ewell, P. T. (2009, November). *Assessment, accountability, and improvement: Revisiting the tension.* (Occasional Paper #1). Champaign, IL: National Institute for Learning Outcomes Assessment. Retrieved from http://www.learningoutcomesassessment.org/documents/ PeterEwell_005.pdf

Johnstone, S. M. (Ed.). (2016). *The Journal of Competency-Based Education.* San Francisco, CA: Western Governors University and John Wiley & Sons.

Klein-Collins, R. (2012a). *Competency-based degree programs in the U.S.: Postsecondary credentials for measurable student learning and performance.* Chicago, IL: Council for Adult and Experiential Learning. Retrieved from http://cdn2.hubspot.net/hubfs/617695/ CAEL_Reports/2012_CompetencyBasedPrograms.pdf

Klein-Collins, R. (2012b). Prior learning assessment: When learning outcomes are what counts. *CAEL Forum and News.* Chicago, IL: Council for Adult and Experiential Learning.

Kuh, G. D. (in press). Getting assessment back on the right track. *CAEL Forum and News: Experiential learning and assessment for today's learner: The link between theory and practice.* Chicago, IL: Council for Adult and Experiential Learning.

Kuh, G. D., Ikenberry, S. O., Jankowski, N. A., Cain, T. R., Ewell, P. T., Hutchings, P., & Kinzie, J. (2015). *Using evidence of student learning to improve higher education.* San Francisco, CA: Jossey-Bass.

Lindquist, J. (1978). *Strategies for change.* Sacramento, CA: Pacific Soundings Press.

Maki, P. (2015). *Assessment that works: A national call, a twenty-first century response.* Washington, DC: Association of American Colleges & Universities.

Mentkowski, M., & Associates. (2000). *Learning that lasts: Integrating learning, development, and performance in college and beyond.* San Francisco, CA: Jossey-Bass.

National Institute of Education. (1984). *Involvement in learning: Realizing the potential of American higher education. Final report of the study group on the conditions of excellence in American higher education.* Washington, DC: Author.

Palomba, C. A., & Banta, T. W. (1999). *Assessment essentials: Planning, implementing, and improving assessment in higher education.* San Francisco, CA: Jossey-Bass.

Rasmussen, K., Northrup, P., & Colson, R. (2017). *Handbook of research on competency-based education in university settings.* Hershey, PA: IGI Global.

Rhodes, T. L., & Finley, A. (2013). *Using the VALUE rubrics for improvement of learning and authentic assessment.* Washington, DC: Association of American Colleges & Universities. Retrieved from https://www.eou.edu/ctl/files/2012/10/E-VALRUBR2.pdf

Rose, A. D., & Leahy, M. A. (1997, Fall). Assessment issues and practices. In A. D. Rose & M. A. Leahy (Eds.), *Assessing adult learning in diverse settings: Current issues and approaches* (pp. 97–100). *New Directions for Adult and Continuing Education*, No. 75. San Francisco, CA: Jossey-Bass.

Sullivan, D. F. (2015). *The VALUE breakthrough: Getting the assessment of student learning in college right.* Washington, DC: Association of American Colleges & Universities.

Tate, P., & Klein-Collins, R. (2015, October). *PLA and CBE on the competency continuum: The relationship between prior learning assessment and competency-based education.* Chicago, IL: Council for Adult and Experiential Learning. Retrieved from http://cdn2.hubspot.net/hubfs/617695/premium_content_resources/CBE-Publications/PDF/CAEL-Views-on-CBE-and-PLA-Oct-2015.pdf

Travers, N. L., & Mandell, A. (Eds.). (launched 2011). *PLA Inside Out: International Journal on Theory, Research and Practice in Prior Learning Assessment.* Saratoga Springs, NY: SUNY Empire State College. Retrieved from http://www.plaio.org/index.php/home/index

Wilbur, G., Marienau, C., & Fiddler, M. (2012). Authenticity for assurance & accountability: Reconnecting standards and qualities for PLA competence & course-based frameworks. *PLA Inside Out: An International Journal on Theory, Research and Practice in Prior Learning Assessment, 1*(2). Retrieved from http://www.plaio.org/index.php/home/article/view/28/55

Younger, D. (2015). Meaningful rigor in portfolio assessment. *The Journal of Continuing and Higher Education, (63)*2, 126–129.

2

FOUNDATIONAL PERSPECTIVES ON LEARNING FROM EXPERIENCE

There is widespread agreement among theorists and practitioners that experience is the basis for all learning (Dewy, 1938; Kolb, 1984, 2015). For education, this philosophy means that "in order to accomplish its ends both for the individual learner and for society, [education] must be based upon experience—which is always the actual life experience of some individual" (Dewey, 1938, p. 89). Learning is the connective tissue between experience and education, which, according to experiential learning theory, is a recurring cycle of transforming experience into learning and learning into knowledge (Kolb, 2015, p. 186). Given that most adults seeking higher learning are rich in experience, learning how to learn from experience needs to be a central objective for higher education (Fiddler, Marienau, & Whitaker, 2006).

Assessment is integral to the process of transforming experience into learning.

> *The process of assessment itself provides a primary opportunity for learning how to learn. Through the feedback process that good assessment provides..., learning can be affirmed, amended, and extended.... From the process perspective [of assessment], awareness of the strengths and weaknesses of the learner's approaches can lead to intentional improvements in the regulation of learning. From the content perspective,*

identifying the quality of the learning provides an essential foundation for setting new objectives that can expand the quantity of learning as well. (Fiddler, Marienau, & Whitaker, 2006, pp. 1–2)

In this chapter, we explore three goals for the assessment of learning from the perspective of theories of learning from experience. These interrelated goals are to (1) elicit genuine learning, (2) foster new learning, and (3) engage critical reflection.

Goal #1: Assessment Processes Can Be Designed to Elicit Genuine Learning

Dewey (1938) posited that two conditions are necessary for genuine learning to occur. First, there needs to be *continuity* so that the person can relate aspects of one experience to another. "Experiences [are] cumulative and the quality of any experience [is] determined by its usefulness in later experiences" (Brewer & Marienau, 2016, p. 407). Dewey's second condition is that there needs to be sufficient *transaction* between the person and her environment to spark some kind of change, either in the process of knowing or the content of what someone knows. Consider the case of Estelle who was raised in South America and lived the Netherlands for two years as a young adult, where she conducted intensive self-study of that country's world-renowned art museums and vibrant local art culture. Having moved to the United States and enrolled in an adult-focused college, was there sufficient continuity in Estelle's transactions with classic and contemporary art for her to be able to test out of one or more art courses? Or, might she prepare a portfolio for prior learning assessment to earn credit or competency in the arts and humanities area?

This adult learner illustrates a common challenge with assessing learning from experience acquired outside of an academic institution. From the perspective of situated learning theory, knowledge acquired in a specific situation may be relevant only in that particular circumstance (Lave & Wenger, 1991).

Estelle's self-guided immersion in the art-culture system most likely met Dewey's conditions for genuine learning. Could she also meet the criteria for college-level learning? The assessment process could help Estelle identify what aspects of her learning might connect to course-based or competency-based outcomes and how she could demonstrate achievement of these outcomes.

Goal #2: Assessment Processes Can Be Designed to Foster New Learning

Adults engage every potential learning experience with brains already crowded with prior experiences. An individual's sense-making of these experiences can either promote or impede new learning. Because prior experiences shape who a person is now and how she understands herself and the world around her, exposure to something new may contradict or expand her established ways of thinking and knowing. Given the strength of an individual's commitment to her filters—ways of seeing and being in the world—those most deeply etched are the most difficult to recognize, let alone change. Mezirow (1991, 2000) surmised that in order to learn, most individuals need to change their perspectives. These *perspective shifts* can be triggered by *disorienting dilemmas*, which concern problems or situations that challenge the person's status quo. Estelle was not learning about art in a familiar context; she was learning to live in a new culture. For example, daily living in Amsterdam presented numerous disorientating dilemmas stemming from dramatic differences in language and customs that required her to change her perspectives. These concepts of disorienting dilemmas and perspective shifts are at the core of Mezirow's theory of *transformational learning*. As the term implies, transformational learning focuses on learning that "liberates adults from distorted perceptions, beliefs, and assumptions that effectively limit their freedom to be responsible actors in the world" (Taylor & Marienau, 2016, p. 273). Though adult life presents a multitude of disorienting dilemmas, many people are adept at working around them, thus avoiding the path toward new learning.

During the assessment process, learners can be challenged to reexamine and question what they know or how they do things. Using Estelle as an example, questions for reflection could focus on *disorienting dilemmas* that she actually experienced while living in Amsterdam. She could also be introduced to theories and models that prompt her to now question what she thought she understood and how she interpreted her experiences. As this case illustrates, the assessment process engages the learner in extracting, examining, and elucidating learning from her experience. The assessment process can help learners develop their capacities for complexity. In Kolb's (1984; 2015) terms, the dimensions of complexity are symbolic (understanding), perceptual (seeing), affective (feeling), and doing (behavioral). In various combinations, these dimensions represent learners' capacities for navigating the demands of adult life (Kegan, 1994) and for engaging in higher order learning.

Goal #3: Assessment Processes Can Be Designed to Engage Learners' Critical Reflection on Their Experience

Adult learners often need prompts, through the process of reflection, to become aware of the learning potential from their experiences. One way to think of reflection is as a "process of inquiry into one's experience" (Fiddler & Marienau, 2008, p. 76). What the act of reflection does is encourage learners to become more conscious of the patterns of the meaning they have already made and to question whether these make sense or need to be altered in light of present circumstances.

However, for the adult learner, the process of extracting learning from experience (prior or current) in ways that can be assessed for higher-order learning is more challenging, both emotionally and cognitively, than many educators may realize. A simplified description of how the brain learns can shed light on this challenge. Every new experience is immediately categorized in terms of something the brain already knows.

Because the brain wants to save energy as it seeks among existing neural patterns, the most frequently used patterns are easier to connect with and will likely take precedence; hence, the tendency is to default to what the individual already knows—the *default pattern* (Taylor & Marienau, 2016). This tendency of the brain may tax learners' cognitive load and inhibit their capacity for critical reflection at the level expected for demonstration of higher-order learning.

When the initial experience (stimulus) is received in the body, the process of categorization includes the emotions connected to the existing neural patterns—the *emotional load*. As the individual starts to make sense of an experience, emotion is always part of the cycle. Indeed, emotions are always part of learning. As Damasio (2000) claims, a person cannot think rationally without emotion. The reality lies not in "I think therefore I am," but in "I feel therefore I know" (Taylor & Marienau, 2016, p. 36). When a learner is asked to identify, interpret, and provide evidence of learning from experience, her emotions will be part of that story. Assessment practices that strive for genuine learning will not shy away from a learner's emotional load; rather, the learner will be supported in reflecting on how her emotions have influenced the way she interprets her experience and the learning she has acquired.

Adults often report that they do not reflect or, more accurately, do not know how to reflect in ways that transform experience into learning (Taylor, Marienau, & Fiddler, 2000). "Effective feedback focuses on developing adults' capacity to revise their own thinking rather than on directing (fixing) their behavior" (Taylor & Marienau, 2016, p. 229). In the assessment process, adult learners need feedback that both affirms what they already know and can do, and guides them to better learning and performance in the future. The kind of feedback most conducive to learning is *facilitative feedback* in the form of "carefully crafted questions that require the adult to rethink rather than just retype" (p. 229). When learners' cognitive and emotional loads are taken into account in the assessment process, genuine learning, along with new learning, can be achieved.

Returning to theories of learning from experience, Dewey directs attention to assessment that centers on genuine learning. Kolb's theory of experiential learning centers assessment on supporting learners in the process of transforming their experience into learning and knowledge. Mezirow's theory of transformative learning encourages using the assessment process to help individuals question, and perhaps change, their meaning-making filters and accustomed behaviors. Lave and Wenger's depiction of situated learning theory raises awareness of the potential limitations of assessing learning only within conventional disciplinary and course-based boundaries. Kuh (2017) reminds us that assessment is intended to be a "quality assurance mechanism" with multiple purposes—to document student learning outcomes, to improve student performance, and to improve institutional performance. These theories about learning from experience provide a solid foundation for intentionally uniting learning and assessment to ensure quality of learning outcomes (current and future) and to provide useful data for the latter purpose.

References

Brewer, P., & Marienau, C. (2016). Maintaining the integrity of portfolio assessment through theoretical understanding. *CAEL Forum & News: Experiential Learning and Assessment for Today's Learner: The Link Between Theory and Practice (in press)*. Chicago, IL: Council for Adult and Experiential Learning.

Brewer, P., & Marienau, C. (2016). The theory and practice of prior learning assessment. In V. C. X. Wang (Ed.), *Theory and practice of adult and higher education* (pp. 399–421). Charlotte, NC: Information Age Publishing.

Damasio, A. R. (2000). *The feeling of what happens: Body and emotion in the making of consciousness*. New York, NY: Harcourt.

Dewey, J. (1938). *Experience and education*. New York, NY: Macmillan.

Fiddler, M., & Marienau, C. (2008). Developing habits of reflection for meaningful learning. S. Reed & C. Marienau (Eds.), *Linking adults with community: Promoting civic engagement through community-based learning* (pp. 75–85). *New Directions for Adult and Continuing Education,* No. 118. San Francisco, CA: Jossey-Bass.

Fiddler, M., Marienau, C., & Whitaker, U. (2006). *Assessing learning: Standards, principles, and procedures* (2nd ed.). Dubuque, IO: Kendall Hunt.

Kegan, R. (1994). *In over our heads: The mental demands of modern life.* Cambridge, MA: Harvard University Press.

Kolb, D. (1984). *Experiential learning: Experience as the source of learning and development.* Englewood Cliffs, NJ: Prentice Hall.

Kolb, D. (2015). *Experiential learning: Experience as the source of learning and development* (2nd ed.). Upper Saddle River, NJ: Pearson Education, Inc.

Kuh, G. D. (2017). Getting assessment back on the right track. *CAEL Forum and News: Experiential Learning and Assessment for Today's Learner: The Link between Theory and Practice.* Chicago, IL: Council for Adult and Experiential Learning. Kuh, G. (in press)

Mezirow, J. (1991). *Transformative dimensions of adult learning.* San Francisco, CA: Jossey-Bass.

Mezirow, J. (2000). *Learning as transformation.* San Francisco, CA: Jossey-Bass.

Taylor, K., & Marienau, C. (2016). *Facilitating learning with the adult brain in mind: A conceptual and practice guide.* San Francisco, CA: Jossey-Bass.

Taylor, K., Marienau, C., & Fiddler, M. (2000). *Developing adult learners: Strategies for teachers and trainers.* San Francisco, CA: Jossey-Bass.

CHAPTER

3 QUALITY STANDARDS FOR ASSESSING LEARNING: A COMMITMENT TO INQUIRING AND DELIBERATING ABOUT ASSESSMENT IN CONTEXT

As noted in Chapter 1, higher education institutions are becoming more intentional and strategic about their commitments to assessment as a core component of the teaching and learning processes. CAEL's 10 Quality Standards provide a framework for institutions to attend to the first commitment—*inquiring and deliberating about assessment in their local context*. A common set of standards helps ensure quality practices across the wide spectrum of organizations and diversity of learners.

This chapter features an updated set of 10 Quality Standards for assessing learning, each of which includes a description of its intention and scope along with certain tensions. Following the collection of Standards is a chart that poses questions institutions might use to guide deliberations and decisions regarding policy and practice. Standards V and VI are new to this third edition. Standard V recognizes that access and equity are critical to students' success. Standard VI recognizes that involvement of learners in their learning, including assessment, is also key to their success. Several other Standards have been reworded to reflect current best practice. For readers who have lived through the history of *Assessing Learning*, or are interested in the evolution of the Standards, we provide a comparison of the 1989 and 2006 Standards at the end of this chapter.

Quality Standards for Assessing Learning

I. Credit or competencies are awarded only for evidence of learning, not for experience or time spent.

Description

This Standard, the cornerstone of learning assessment, requires that institutions focus on the demonstrated results (i.e., outcomes) of a given learning process. The operative term in this Standard is *evidence*—of the individual having gained knowledge and/or skill that meet criteria established by the entity awarding the credit or competency. Documentation of experience does not always provide evidence of learning. Learning becomes assessable when the documentation not only shows that the learner actually participated in the experiences, but also *and only* when the learner demonstrates convincingly the learning that is represented in the documentation. It is common practice to use the terms *documentation* and *evidence* interchangeably, but doing so masks the emphasis on the demonstration of learning that sits at the center of quality assessment.

Evidence of learning, especially with regard to prior learning, can take various forms, for example, work artifacts, research reports, performances, symbolic representations, and interviews. Methods for assessing students' evidence of learning may include departmental challenge exams (i.e., credit by exam); national standardized exams (e.g., Advanced Placement, CLEP, UExcel, DSST); credit recommendations via American Council on Education (ACE) and LearningCounts. org; CAEL's evaluation of portfolios; or individual institutional evaluation of portfolios. A portfolio approach can work well especially for different forms of evidence and particularly when presented in some combination. Regardless of form and format, in order for credit or competency to be awarded, evidence(s) of learning must align with the stated criteria and procedures.

Thus, this Standard requires assessment of actual evidence, not inference based on claimed experiences or how long the individual was engaged in doing something. The intention of this Standard was established over four decades ago and is reinforced in this volume.

II. Assessment is integral to learning because it leads to and enables future learning.

Description

Experience per se does not always or necessarily lead to learning. As explained in Chapter 2, reflection on the part of the learner is the precursor to interpreting experience and transforming it into learning. Assessment may ultimately lead to decisions about where students should be placed or how much credit should be awarded for external institutional learning. However, when made integral to learning, assessment is not just a score but also a feedback loop that allows for more learning.

Both formative and summative assessments are a critical part of the learning process. Summative assessment occurs at the end of a unit or program, serving as assessment *of* learning. A formative assessment approach features assessment *for* learning, where learners are offered facilitated feedback as their learning proceeds to help them revise their thinking or means of expression. Ideally, formative assessment engages learners as partners in an iterative process of reflecting on what has been learned in one context and transferring to another. Self-assessment typically focuses on the person's experience of being a learner, beyond the material or content.

Optimally, assessment helps the learner generate not just knowing more about what is already familiar, but also seeing things in a new way. Assessment that enables future learning involves both assessment *for* learning (formative) and assessment *of* learning, or the results (summative). Assessment is most powerful when it is incorporated into the ongoing work of learning and teaching, not treated as a separate add-on.

III. Assessment is based on criteria for outcomes that are clearly articulated and shared among constituencies.

Description

While each of the Standards reinforces various aspects of quality in assessing learning, this Standard is pivotal. When criteria for learning outcomes are clearly articulated and communicated among all stakeholders, quality thrives; when addressed insufficiently, quality suffers. "Experience is an input and learning is an outcome; credit [or competency] awards must be based on the latter" (Fiddler, Marienau, & Whitaker, 2006, p. 14). The outcomes should indicate the level of learning to be achieved (e.g., college-level or higher-level indicators that represent agreed upon definitions).

Outcomes based on criteria encompass three critical components. First, assessment, whether formative or summative, is dependent on indicators of progress toward a predetermined endpoint (that may represent varying degrees of specificity). Second, these criteria are to be thoughtfully derived from carefully selected sources—whether from existing curricula, from industry-professional standards, or constructed anew by institutional representatives, and/or in partnership with each learner. Third, these criteria need to be carefully and clearly expressed because they are intended to be used by everyone involved in the assessment process: advisors, assessors, learners, transcript recipients.

What these components mean, in practice, is that there is a clear process of articulating criteria through deliberation and consensus among relevant subject matter experts (see also Standard IV). In addition, this deliberative process needs to be owned by the institution so that the resulting criteria are an expression of the institution's standards and distinct character. Increasingly, faculty are reexamining learning outcomes in existing courses, so the outcomes are measurable in terms of content, levels of learning, and connection with outcomes of other courses.

The guidelines for awarding credit need to represent clearly stated criteria and, at the same time, recognize individuals' learning experiences as variable. Often the focus of the institution is on designing learning experiences—the inputs—with somewhat less attention to thoughtfully choosing ways to determine the outputs of learning through assessment. The process of developing criteria and rubrics may bring the two into balance.

IV. The determination of credit awards and competency levels are made by appropriate subject matter and credentialing experts.

Description

This Standard is crucial to issues of quality and equity in learning assessment. Academic credit and professional designations are based on demonstrated learning and/or skill that depends on the judgment of experts. Within the academy, the experts are the faculty. On occasions when students present evidence of learning in subject matters not represented among the faculty, external content experts may be consulted. Without expert judgment, credit decisions could be indiscriminate—based on general, sometimes superficial, understanding of the meaning and intention of assessment criteria and little if any understanding of the context in which they would be applied. A generalist might understand if a student's treatment of a learning outcome is relevant, but only a subject matter expert will be able to determine if it is sufficient and accurate. In disciplinary-oriented programs, only the faculty know their field's distinctive questions, methods, and ways of thinking that will inform assessment of student learning. In addition, the award of credit or its equivalent should be informed by credentialing experts who know the basis for particular credentials (e.g., industry certifications, continuing education units (CEUs), microcredentials, such as badges) and, therefore, are able to responsibly apply them within the boundaries of the institution or organization.

V. Assessment advances the broader purpose of access and equity for diverse individuals and groups to support their success.

Description

At first glance, assessment may not seem to be a major player if the goals of access and equity are perceived mainly as reaching out to and bringing in diverse learners. However, this new Standard recognizes that access extends far beyond getting students through the front door of our institutions, into the physical space. Access also entails a hospitable environment that is conducive to effective learning throughout students' studies with the institution. Equity involves offering variable opportunities for learning and recognizing evidence of learning that is congruent with the individual learner while leading toward learning outcomes. Access and equity work hand in hand to foster students' success.

Within the context of assessment, an essential factor in promoting the aims of access, equity, and success resides in Standard III: clearly articulated criteria for learning outcomes that are visible to all parties. These criteria need to be not only *clear* but also *flexible* in terms of accommodating multiple forms of evidence. The attendant assessment practices need to be *empathic* in the sense of respecting a range of contexts for learning and diverse perspectives. Further, assessment needs to be carried out with *integrity*—experts consistently applying relevant criteria in an accurate, transparent, and constructive manner. When the criteria for learning outcomes make room for the voice and context of each individual, when multiple forms of evidence of learning are supported, and when the right experts are examining learning outcomes in the right way, the pathway is cleared toward advancing access and equity for diverse learners.

VI. Institutions proactively provide guidance and support for learners' full engagement in the assessment process.

Description

This new Standard focuses explicitly on institutions proactively engaging and supporting students in assessment processes. Students should be regarded as central actors in, not just objects of, assessment. One way to treat students as partners in learning is through self-assessment when it emphasizes having them monitor and adjust their own performance and, over time, direct their own learning beyond a discrete outcome. Self-assessment can be incorporated into any method of learning assessment. It is especially relevant in the process of assessing prior learning, and portfolio assessment in particular, given the importance of the learner's reflections and self-explanations. Students could partner in the learning assessment process in other ways. This participation might entail their having a voice in the criteria that will be used for assessing their work, or it might entail involving students in selecting tools for assessment, for example choosing between a standardized test or a portfolio.

In order for students to be partners in assessment, they need to understand the terminology, policies, and options that are related to the assessment of learning in its various forms. Guidance and support are needed at all stages of the educational journey, from pre-admission through graduation, and so many people in various roles at an institution have a hand in assessment. Support for students certainly should involve the provision of clear and complete information in multiple media as well as advising, screening, coaching, and/or instruction in how to choose assessment methods best suited to them as learners and to their educational goals. Most adult learners benefit from instruction in how to do meaningful self-assessment and to assume co-ownership for assessment of their learning.

VII. Assessment policies and procedures are the result of inclusive deliberation and are shared with all constituencies.

Description

In order for learning assessment to impact students' success, their equitable and active involvement in assessment (Standards V & VI) must be well integrated into the institution's structures, systems, and consciousness of all of its constituents. The increased focus on assessment that has emerged over the past 20 years or so has led institutions to expand their assessment approaches and practices and the related administrative procedures. It is tempting to simply add new services, but doing so without ensuring that they are well connected to existing ones may marginalize their impact. For example, assessment of general education became one of those new practices that institutions began to implement. In some institutions, such assessment was added as a discrete function and as one among many elements in the institution's required quality assurance procedures. In other institutions, in contrast, general education assessment has been integrated into the process of program review, course evaluations, and the development of new curricula, thereby reinforcing its value to the quality of educational programming. In the same way, assessment of prior learning needs to be fully integrated into the institution's overall approach to the student's learning journey.

Further, because learning occurs inside and outside the classroom, as well as outside of the institution, policies and practices must be robust enough to encompass that spectrum and ideally result from collaboration among a broad range of stakeholders, including those from the workplace. At minimum, this collaboration is grounded in a shared philosophy of the educational value of assessment that is then enacted in the policies and procedures the group articulates. The "inclusive deliberation" that generates practical assessment guidelines and criteria discussed in Standard III contributes to a positive climate for assessment. Inclusive deliberation also does much to advance a more embedded culture of assessment within the institution by valuing the experience and perspectives of various stakeholders.

VIII. Fees charged for assessment are based on the services performed in the process rather than the credit awarded.[1]

Description

This Standard is intended to ensure both the integrity and the sustainability of the institution's assessment services. Credit-based tuition is predicated on the full service of the institution, including curriculum development, instruction, and assessment. By developing a similar fee structure for assessment that is predicated on the cost of delivering and supporting that assessment, the institution can ensure its capacity to comply with this Standard and provide sufficient assessment options for its students. Fees for assessment should be clearly linked to assessment services, and should be used to support them and communicate that the institution regards assessment as an essential component of the academic process. When determining a fee structure that will ensure the quality of assessment, transactional costs, such as compensation to faculty assessors, must be considered if the institution chooses to do prior learning assessment in-house rather than use CAEL's LearningCounts.org service. Any in-house program must also consider fixed costs, such as having a dedicated assessment office and staff. Still other expenses may be more integrated into the larger system, such as recruitment, technology support, and professional development. While establishing fees

---

[1] Updates to this Standard were informed largely by *PLA Is Your Business* by Rebecca Klein-Collins, copyright 2015, November, CAEL.

that will adequately support assessment services, the institution should beware of creating conflicts of interest for itself through revenue incentives. The tension between providing realistic support for assessment services and ensuring opportunities for students to participate in assessment is best managed through frequent and data-informed review. Institutions that use a fee structure based on credits awarded run the risk of being perceived as selling credits without adequate service or educational value.

IX. All practitioners involved in the assessment process pursue and receive adequate training and continuing professional development for the functions they perform.

Description

Assessment is a specialized role for faculty as are curriculum development and instruction. Although many educators view assessment as loosely embedded in the instructional process, assessment of learning is distinct from teaching. It is a subfield with its own philosophies, standards, and best practices—which this volume attempts to address. Engaging faculty in assessment is a challenge in many institutions, not because faculty do not want to enhance and improve student learning outcomes but because assessment is sometimes just one more major initiative to be subsumed in crowded responsibilities. In order to mitigate against "assessment fatigue," faculty and all other stakeholders in the institution need incentives and rewards to invest in building another area of capability. And, just as educators are committed to continuous learning in their disciplines and fields, they need to include assessment in their ongoing learning agenda. While some individuals or groups may be designated as the in-house experts and custodians of assessment, anyone who interacts with assessment of learning is obliged to learn as much as possible about it.

This Standard speaks not only to educators needing to seek opportunities to learn about assessment but also to improve their practice in assessment. In reciprocal fashion, the Standard speaks to the institution, which needs to provide ample opportunities for initial and continuing training and development in learning assessment.

X. Assessment programs are regularly monitored, evaluated, and revised to respond to institutional and learner needs.

Description

The burgeoning focus on outcomes in both higher education and workplace contexts, fueled by the competency-based movement, compels assessment programs to be agile and responsive to changing program requirements and learner needs. Assessment programs need to stay current with changes in curriculum and delivery structures, in policies issued by federal and accrediting bodies, and in the expanding knowledge base that informs assessment. Assessment programs need to be monitored and evaluated to determine whether and how well the intended learning outcomes are being achieved. Reviews might be targeted on a particular area, such as Standard V, which signals the need for persistent attention to how assessment practices support the aims of access and equity and, ultimately, students' success. Review and revision of assessment programs need not, and should not, wait for formal institutional evaluation cycles, which tend to come around every 7–10 years.

To promote better approaches to learning assessment, many institutions have established institution-wide "teaching, learning, and assessment" (TLA) centers, and some units have local TLA committees. The TLA entities may be best suited to monitor assessment policies and practices on a regular basis and conduct targeted reviews of specific components that can be revised or created on an as-needed basis.

Standards and Questions to Guide Deliberations & Decisions

In the spirit of deliberative decision-making, we pose questions to help guide conversations about implementation of the 10 Standards. Institutional leaders can approach the answers to these questions by examining the extent to which current policies and practices meet the Standards and considering what aspects call for creation or improvement.

TABLE 1.

Standards	Questions to Guide Deliberations & Decisions
I. Credit or competencies are awarded only for evidence of learning and not for experience or time spent.	How open are our policies to recognizing learning whenever and wherever it has occurred (i.e., to what extent does the source of learning matter)?
	How do we define college-level or higher-level learning?
	How are faculty and staff encouraged to consider and use multiple assessment methods for various types of learning?
	In what ways does the discipline/field influence what we identify as appropriate evidence of learning?
	How are courses designed to rely on varied forms of evidence for students to demonstrate the learning outcomes?
	What is the rationale for considering learning from nonaccredited programs, noncredit programs that may be college level, for credit or competency award?
II. Assessment is integral to learning because it leads to and enables future learning.	In what ways are formative assessment and feedback used across the curriculum?
	How do students and faculty use students' self-assessments to foster new learning?
	Under what conditions can a student revise work for re-assessment?
	What guidance do faculty receive in how to provide effective feedback to students that addresses a variety of learning purposes?
	How do faculty assessors learn to make decisive judgments about credit/competency awards?
	Is there a role for common scoring rubrics? Might these be homegrown or external (e.g., LEAP's VALUE rubrics, CAEL's LearningCounts)?

(Continued)

Standards	Questions to Guide Deliberations & Decisions
III. Assessment is based on criteria for outcomes that are clearly articulated and shared among constituencies.	What role do part-time and full-time faculty have in determining learning outcomes at the program level?
	What ensures that our learning outcomes align with the environment where they will be applied?
	How do faculty learn how to identify and articulate criteria for assessment?
	How will rubrics be used to further elaborate the criteria? At what level of specificity?
	Who are the stakeholders for our learning outcomes, and how are they involved in creating or reviewing them?
IV. The determination of credit awards and competency levels are made by appropriate subject matter and credentialing experts.	What roles can outside experts play in the assessment of learning? What rationale is required to gain approval for their involvement?
	How are outside experts oriented to program assessment practices?
	How do subject matter experts learn to use their expertise for purposes of assessment and not just for instruction?
V. Assessment advances the broader purpose of access and equity for diverse individuals and groups to support their success.	Which of our assessment policies have the potential to limit or expand access for diverse or traditionally underserved learners?
	How do our admission criteria and assessment measures accommodate learners of varied life backgrounds and academic abilities?
	How might PLA advance or impede equity?
	How might competency-based assessment approaches advance or impede equity?
	How do faculty and staff learn to balance being gatekeepers of standards with being ambassadors for alternate pathways to meet the standards?
VI. Institutions proactively provide guidance and support for learners' full engagement in the assessment process.	To what extent and in what ways are students seen as partners in assessment or simply as recipients of assessment services?
	What opportunities do our students have in selecting tools and strategies to assess their learning?
	In what ways do our programs orient and reinforce students' capabilities to self-assess?
	What kinds of services help students prepare for participation in assessment and support them in the process?
	What is the distinction between supporting students' participation in assessment and coaching them to earn credit? To what extent is coaching acceptable in our assessment practice?

(Continued)

Standards	Questions to Guide Deliberations & Decisions
VII. Assessment policies and procedures are the result of inclusive deliberation and are shared with all constituencies.	What processes do our departments use to ensure that course learning outcomes reflect general consensus by faculty who teach the course? What governance and/or administrative structures guide the involvement of stakeholders in creating assessment policy and practice? What means of communication are used to inform all constituencies, including students, of assessment policies and procedures? How does our assessment policy either cultivate or discourage a healthy climate for assessing learning? How do we or can we support faculty and staff in ways that energize their participation in assessment rather than generates fatigue and skepticism?
VIII. Fees charged for assessment are based on the services performed in the process rather than the credit awarded.	What is the institution's business model for assessment: cost recovery, loss leader for recruitment, generating additional revenue, outsourcing to a third party? What existing policies or agreements inform the specific decisions regarding fees to be charged and compensation to be paid in the assessment process? What direct and indirect costs are considered when we establish assessment fees?
IX. All practitioners involved in the assessment process pursue and receive adequate training and continuing professional development for the functions they perform.	Are the roles and functions associated with assessment defined clearly for all parties? In what ways are faculty, staff, and administrators provided with training from assessment experts? How do individuals and groups learn to carry out their specialized functions in assessment? How are experienced individuals utilized to teach/train others?
X. Assessment programs are regularly monitored, evaluated, and revised to respond to institutional and learner needs.	How well aligned are elements of assessment with overall institutional goals? What questions guide our evaluation of the assessment enterprise? What approaches are being used to review and evaluate assessment operations? What role do faculty and staff play in program evaluation efforts?

Shifts in Quality Standards

In the three editions of *Assessing Learning*, CAEL's intention has been to hold the Quality Standards as constant as possible while updating them to accommodate shifts in higher education in the broader social context. The image of a compass (the kind from geometry class, see Figure 1) may illustrate the balance between consistency and change.

© *Victor Metelskiy/Shutterstock.com*

Fig. 1 Compass

Responsible practitioners want both consistent quality (the fixed point) and flexible processes (the movable leg) to ensure that assessment is committed to broad principles that capture the nature of learning across settings. We can adjust the assessment procedures so that they fit organizations, populations, purposes, and resources, but the range of those procedures is limited by the fixed point of quality standards. Of course, in geometry class we also learned when to move the compass to relocate its stationary leg and, thereby, adjust the range of the movable leg.

Consider the following table that shows a comparison among the three versions of the Standards: 1989, 2006, and 2017. The initial Standards were asserting the validity of a relatively new and often misunderstood academic practice: prior learning assessment. The language of the Standards made strong, clear statements that implied "right" and "wrong" ways of conducting prior learning assessment. In 2006, the Standards had been in use for 17 years. The second edition clarified that the Standards were intended to inform the assessment of learning generally; though, practitioners often relied on them primarily for guidance in the practice of PLA. The confusion is understandable. The 2017 Standards recognize that over the past decades, numerous innovations, tools, successes, and failures have illuminated additional needs for guidance. Assessing learning has been recognized to encompass more than prior learning and to have ownership beyond higher education (e.g., in the workplace). Alternative practices will continue to emerge that challenge existing definitions of quality and standards and lead to future shifts.

TABLE 2. *EVOLUTION OF CAEL STANDARDS FOR ASSESSING LEARNING*

1989	2006	2017
I. Credit should be awarded only for learning and not for experience.	I. Credit or its equivalent should be awarded only for learning, and not for experience. *Comment: "Its equivalent" is a stand in for competency, which had not yet gained recognition in higher education.*	I. Credit or competencies are awarded only for evidence of learning and not for experience or time spent. *Comment: The term competencies is added to reflect the growth of competency-based education across higher education. "Time spent" is added to signal two common but bad practices—awarding credit/competencies on the basis of having the experience and/or length of time involved in the experience.*
II. College credit should be awarded only for college-level learning.	II. Assessment should be based on standards and criteria for the level of acceptable learning that are both agreed upon and made public. *Comment: The Standard was broadened beyond "college-level" to encompass learning in other contexts such as the workplace. Also, inclusion of "agreed upon and made public" was intended to put the onus of defining college-level learning on the institution.*	II. Assessment is integral to learning because it leads to and enables future learning. *Comment: This framing further elevates the learning potential that assessment can support and accentuates the recent move away from compliance and toward learning. This Standard is a re-articulation of the 2006 Standard III.*
III. Credit should be awarded only for learning that has a balance, appropriate to the subject, between theory and practical application.	III. Assessment should be treated as an integral part of learning, not separate from it, and should be based on an understanding of learning processes. *Comment: The 1989 version reflects the concern at the time about prior learning being too practically oriented at the expense of theory. By 2006, this issue had received substantive attention. Assessment was gaining recognition as an essential element of the learning process.*	III. Assessment is based on criteria for outcomes that are clearly articulated and shared among constituencies. *Comment: This framing emphasizes the importance of outcomes as an essential guide for assessment. It also incorporates the notion of transparency (2006 Standard II).*

(Continued)

1989	2006	2017
IV. The determination of competence levels and of credit awards must be made by appropriate subject matter and academic experts.	IV. The determination of credit awards and competence levels must be made by appropriate subject matter and academic or credentialing experts. *Comment: "Credentialing" experts were added as higher education began to expand the pool of experts whose opinion could help inform judgments made by the faculty.*	IV. The determination of credit awards and competency levels are made by appropriate subject matter and credentialing experts. *Comment: No significant change from 2006.*
V. Credit should be appropriate to the academic context in which it is accepted.	V. Credit or other credentialing should be appropriate to the context in which it is awarded and accepted. *Comment: "Other credentialing," at that time, referred subtly to competence.*	V. Assessment advances the broader purpose of access and equity for diverse individuals and groups to support their success. *Comment: This new Standard represents the increasing diversity of learners in higher education and the critical role that access and equity play in their success. Feedback from educators indicated that the 1989 and 2006 Standard V concerning credit "appropriate to the context" was too obvious; hence, this Standard has been retired.*
VI. Credit awards and their transcript entries should be monitored to avoid giving credit twice for the same learning.	VI. If awards are for credit, transcript entries should clearly describe what learning is being recognized and should be monitored to avoid giving credit twice for the same learning.	VI. Institutions proactively provide guidance and support for learners' full engagement in the assessment process. *Comment: This new Standard recognizes that when the aim of assessment is to foster learning, students must be engaged in the process. Feedback from educators indicated that the 1989 and 2006 Standard VI has become common practice; hence, this Standard has been retired.*

(Continued)

1989	2006	2017
VII. Policies and procedures applied to assessment, including provision for appeal, should be fully disclosed and prominently available.	VII. Policies, procedures, and criteria applied to assessment, including provision for appeal, should be fully disclosed and prominently available to all parties involved in the assessment process.	VII. Assessment policies and procedures are the result of inclusive deliberation and are shared with all constituencies. *Comment: This framing consolidates the specific points made in the 1989 and 2006 Standard VII.*
VIII. Fees charged for assessment should be based on the services performed in the process and not determined by the amount of credit awarded.	VIII. Fees charged for assessment should be based on the services performed in the process and not determined by the amount of credit awarded.	VIII. Fees charged for assessment are based on the services performed in the process rather than the credit awarded. *Comment: No change; determining the fee structure for assessment of learning continues to be a major challenge for many institutions.*
IX. All personnel involved in the assessment of learning should receive adequate training for the functions they perform, and there should be provision for their continued professional development.	IX. All personnel involved in the assessment of learning should pursue and receive adequate training and continuing professional development for the functions they perform. *Comment: "Should pursue" was intended to encourage faculty and others to be proactive in learning about assessment and how to do it. In other words, professional development is the responsibility of both the institution and the faculty.*	IX. All practitioners involved in the assessment process pursue and receive adequate training and continuing professional development for the functions they perform. *Comment: No change.*
X. Assessment programs should be regularly monitored, reviewed, evaluated, and revised as needed to reflect changes in the needs being served and in the state of the assessment arts.	X. Assessment programs should be regularly monitored, reviewed, evaluated, and revised as needed to reflect changes in the needs being served, the purposes being met, and the state of the assessment arts.	X. Assessment programs are regularly monitored, evaluated, and revised to respond to institutional and learner needs. *Comment: No substantive change.*

In most any context, a set of standards is intended to assure reasonable consistency in practice and to represent contemporary values of the relevant field. To ensure that the field is able to evolve, standards must be both developed and used so that they assure stability but do not encourage stagnation. As noted above, the standards for assessing learning were revised as priorities and values of the field changed, in effect moving the "compass" that demonstrates the relationship between standards (the fixed leg) and practices (the movable leg). Considering practice that is responsive both to quality standards and to the institutional context depends on deliberation within the institution. The following chapter highlights particular assessment practices and how the selection of assessment practices may honor institutional characteristics and priorities.

References

Fiddler, M., Marienau, C., & Whitaker, U. (2006). *Assessing learning: Standards, principles, & procedures* (2nd ed.). Dubuque, IO: Kendall Hunt.

Whitaker, U. (1989). *Assessing learning: Standards, principles, & procedures* (1st ed.). Columbia, MD: CAEL

4 ALIGNING PRACTICES WITH PURPOSES: A COMMITMENT TO ALIGNING ASSESSMENT PRACTICES WITH INSTITUTIONAL PURPOSES

As a key component of the learning process and of learning systems, assessment always resides within a context and is directed to serve particular purposes, such as awarding credit, providing feedback to the student for educational purposes, and placement. Assessing student learning within a course determines whether or not the student will receive credit and often what grade will be awarded. An assessment of program level outcomes provides feedback to the institution about the success of the program in achieving its educational purpose. Assessing students' writing and math skills upon admission determines the optimal course placement to support their academic success. And the list goes on. Assessment offers tools used by advisors, faculty, and administrators to gather information about student ability and achievement to serve a wide range of institutional purposes. Given the richness of assessment tools and applications, identifying promising practices can be daunting. We have chosen to do so within the context of several key purposes familiar to higher education institutions of all types and to many organizations outside of higher education.

The following four categories each identify a general institutional purpose that relies on information resulting from the thoughtful and strategic assessment of student learning. The purposes collectively address the full scope of the institution: the facilitation of learning, the meaningful design of programs, tools, and services, and the development and execution of institutional policy. There certainly are others, and readers are invited to identify additional purposes and the relationship of assessment to each.

In this chapter, we look at specific ways that assessment contributes to:

- **Assessment Purpose 1: Development of Individuals**—directing programs and services to the full development of learners, both within and beyond the scope of explicit academic standards.

- **Assessment Purpose 2: Serving Adults Intentionally**—determining the attributes and needs of today's post-traditional students to guide the meaningful design of programs and services.

- **Assessment Purpose 3: Relevant Transfer of Learning**—ensuring that the expectations of the workplace and other external contexts are aligned with academic standards and assessment practices.

- **Assessment Purpose 4: Ensuring Consistent Practice Across Institutions**—convening subject matter and credentialing experts to build consensus about the treatment of noncollegiate learning, including the means of transcription of credit awards and conditions for the transfer of PLA credit.

For each of these institutional purposes, we have identified several assessment practices that demonstrate how assessment may serve broader institutional priorities as well as specific programmatic needs. The general practices we identify in relation to each purpose are considered promising because they lend themselves to implementation in an array of specific settings and institutional types. Each of these practices may be designed to use particular tools or approaches that customize assessment to institutions, populations, organizational structures, and disciplines.

Institutional Purpose 1:
The Development of Individuals

Higher education aspires to "draw out" of individuals their potential to be effective workers, active citizens, and caring family members and friends. What role does assessment have in this enterprise? Beyond certifying that particular levels of achievement have been met, accompanied by credit or not, assessment offers insight to individuals about their tendencies, processes, talents, and histories as well as about their knowledge, skills, and abilities. It is tempting to think of assessment in operational terms, given its critical role in certifying learning and justifying the award of credentials. This role is typically assessment in competency-based education (CBE). An intentional focus on the development of individuals, however, also invokes the *formative power* of assessment and its link to the aspiration of higher education. As a strong voice for liberal education, the Association of American Colleges & Universities advocates preparing students to "understand and manage complexity, diversity, and change" and to "learn how to apply knowledge and skills in real-world settings" (2015, p. 1). These aims are congruent with competency-based *learning* (CBL) which assessment practices can help accentuate and achieve. As noted in the discussion of Standard II ("Assessment is integral to learning because it leads to and enables future learning,") formative assessment puts the accent on learning and on the potential for students to not only learn more about the same but to see and know differently (Taylor & Marienau, 2016, p. 291). The learner is invited into the realm of higher-order thinking and, optimally, acting responsibly in the world.

The notion of developing individuals implies addressing the whole person and not just "drawing out" the cognitive dimensions directly related to academic credit. Many institutions now include student development competencies among their learning outcomes; these "high-level transferable skills" include "communication, evidence-based reasoning, and problem-solving" (AAC&U, 2015, p. 1). The pathway to developing many of these abilities involves learner engagement in co-curricular activities and feedback from peers, advisors, and staff to gauge their growth in these areas. For many adult students, these abilities are cultivated through professional, vocational, and civic engagement prior to and during college, rather than through co-curricular programs since it is common for adult students to spend little time on campus beyond attending classes. Assessment becomes the vehicle for identifying nonacademic abilities and helping adult students appreciate their relevance to both school and other life domains.

While formative assessment is an important tool for the development of all learners, it has particular power for those with less higher education experience and who may have never seen themselves as "college material." For these students, the opportunity for feedback, both affirming and constructively critical, is an essential ingredient of persistence. The focus on the process of discovery and learning that is underscored by formative assessment provides important context for the results of summative assessment, regardless of the outcome. The transitions associated with entry into college and the milestones along the way are eased when it becomes apparent to learners that an array of personal attributes and abilities contributes to their education, far beyond those linked to the specific academic criteria for which they are held accountable by the institution's programs. Formative assessment may help adult learners understand and appreciate that their career expertise and accomplishments have led them to hone certain abilities, while other abilities that are valued in academics have yet to be fully developed.

The development of adult students is enabled by educational policies, structures, and approaches that take the individual learner into account. At the heart of each of the general practices that follow is the premise that engaging the uniqueness of the individual within academic activities holds great promise for development of the whole person. The following three general assessment practices support the development of individuals as well as provide examples of assessment tools or strategies that may be used in relation to each.

Practice 1 for Developing Individuals: Preparation and Support for Engaging in Assessment

Responsible and effective assessment depends upon the involvement of the learner to varying degrees and in a variety of ways. Students often need to learn how to play their part in the assessment enterprise. Beyond the actual assessment of learning, the processes institutions use to help students prepare for assessment often have profound impact on the development of the individual student. Whether the assessment method involves testing, performance demonstration, or portfolio evaluation; students are asked to take stock of their skills, experiences, and tendencies prior to the actual assessment so they can represent their abilities as fully as possible. For example, students who self-identify as "poor test takers" may discover through a brush-up workshop or session with a coach that they have specific difficulties with testing rather than deficiencies in comprehension of the material. Changing their self-perception can change their mental and emotional states as they approach testing, permitting them to better reflect what they know on the test. In general, preparation for assessment leads learners to develop a richer understanding of their relationship with education, enabling them to make better choices and to more accurately represent their abilities and potential.

For example, support staff for students who are developing portfolios to submit for PLA credit may engage them in a systematic review of life work and experiences as well as reflection on the meaning and impact of those experiences. The results of that review will inform the contents of the portfolio. In addition, students' recognition of past accomplishments, patterns in behavior, and personal attributes may also prompt them to refresh or correct their self-images. The narrative that constitutes the centerpiece of a PLA portfolio captures the information and reflection necessary to demonstrate learning for credit, while the process of writing the narrative may serve as an exercise in self-discovery.

Portfolios are used in a variety of ways in higher education as a means of collecting evidence of the student's ability within a course, across a degree program, or as an option within PLA. In some cases, portfolios are used for particular student development purposes because of the power of the narrative in helping individuals reflect upon and better understand themselves. Narrative is especially potent in empowering those who perceive themselves as misfits in college because their path to and through college is considered by some as unconventional and challenging to the structures of higher education. Most adult and other post-traditional learners experience some sense of not fitting in, unless they are members of a program or college that is designed intentionally and exclusively for adults. Creating narrative with the kind of richness that generates insight and provokes change does not come naturally to many people. In the course of doing business or managing one's life, people are encouraged to draw conclusions quickly and to be efficient rather than expansive or change-oriented. Portfolio development courses and coaching sessions can prompt learners to reflect and to see connections among experiences; otherwise, they might look for simple answers to deep questions such as: *What is the relationship of experience to learning? What does college level mean? What was the primary takeaway from an experience or phase of life? What is the significance of this for present and future endeavors?* By urging learners to create timelines, identify key events, write learning autobiographies, and recognize relevant evidence of past learning, support for portfolio development can stimulate growth in individuals as they present their case to the college that they have achieved college-level learning from past experiences.

Whether used to collect exemplars of professional or vocational competency or to provide a student's case for prior learning credit, portfolios are predicated on the student's role in interpreting and expressing competency in a particular context. In constructing a portfolio within a course or program structure, students exercise their judgment in selecting artifacts that they consider exemplary and are called on to explain the criteria that led to that decision. Portfolios developed for prior learning assessment are guided by criteria provided by the institution. Students then interpret and apply these criteria in making the case that the learning they achieved outside of or before they entered the institution is equivalent to academic requirements. In doing so, adult learners serve a critical role in demonstrating the link between academic programs and demands of the workplace and the community. It is to the institution's benefit, as well as the student's, to prepare adult learners to fully engage in developing portfolios.

Practice 2 for Developing Individuals: Using Qualitative Feedback

Feedback is integral to formative assessment and can be incorporated into summative assessment as well. Because it is a social interaction, feedback needs to be calibrated to the individual learner. Feedback is effective when it is offered in a way such that the individual is able to hear it and be open to possibilities for revising her or his work. The following *Qualities of Assessment* have guided faculty in the competency-based programs in the School for New Learning at DePaul University for over two decades. These qualities can be applied to any setting in which qualitative narrative feedback is used (Younger et al., 2000).

- *Clarity* stresses communicating clear expectations by articulating criteria for the demonstration of competence or outcomes.
- *Flexibility* promotes assessment of learning through multiple forms of evidence. Multiple ways of knowing and learning are honored in demonstrating competence and can be identified in the exchange between learner and assessor in the feedback process.
- *Empathy* embraces individual perspectives and the context of their learning. We respect the diverse voices that inform experience, reducing the privileged position of the academic authority. We recognize and seek to integrate the social, emotional, and intellectual dimensions of learning.
- *Integrity* focuses on applying transparent criteria and indicators of quality in assessing learning in an honest,

accurate, and constructive manner. Integrity relies on informed expertise for assessment and critically examines who and how the expert is identified.

Feedback can take different forms; each should be used with intention. *Directive feedback* instructs (tells) the student on what to do; *corrective feedback* essentially involves editing, whether of written words or behaviors; *facilitative feedback* poses carefully crafted questions that invite the person to think through things for themselves (See Taylor & Marienau, 2016, pp. 229–230). Facilitative feedback tends to be the most effective for fostering further learning and change. Many adults, having been socialized through school and work, associate feedback with the "bleeding red pen phenomenon" which focuses largely on the corrective feedback emphasis on "what is wrong." The antennae of adult brains are especially sensitive to what they perceive as negative feedback and, without a healthy sprinkling of "what is right," may tune out and turn off.

These qualities of assessment and the forms of feedback can function whether the context is a course, a portfolio, a structured interview, a product assessment, or a performance evaluation. Using feedback templates, whether written or oral, is a good practice because a template helps with consistency and fairness while still allowing for personalized commentary. Rubrics for assessment can be used in a formative way to help learners, individually and with peers, gauge their progress during a course or performance period at work. When feedback is used in formative ways, the summative assessment can be a synopsis of what has transpired with no surprises at the end for the learner.

Practice 3 for Developing Individuals: Encouraging Self-Assessment

Self-assessment is a form of reflection that means "to sit beside oneself…" This practice requires, metaphorically, being in two places at once—as both an "actor and an observer and evaluator of those actions" (Taylor & Marienau, 2016, p. 222).

Self-assessment invites students to weigh in with a perspective about their own past performance, current level of ability, and aspirations for the future. Engaging in self-assessment can encourage individuals to seek feedback from others which, in turn, enhances their learning and performance and can even improve their interpersonal relationships (Marienau, 1999).

When self-assessment is integrated into other assessment activities, it is a data source that contributes to assessment decisions regarding credit or other metrics. At best, self-assessment results are reviewed by faculty and advisors and become the basis for ongoing conversation that honors the student as a stakeholder, rather than a recipient, in his or her own education. Given its potential power, self-assessment should be highly valued and that value clearly communicated to students through how it is incorporated into the educational experience.

Tools, prompts, and processes that engage adults in self-assessment are most effective when they are framed to reference specific experiences and to stimulate reflection, rather than describing and reporting what happened. Prompt questions from the facilitator that ask learners to make deeper connections with the material and more meaningful applications in their lives can foster metacognitive abilities. As adult learners become more practiced with self-assessment, they begin to pose their own prompt questions. Another way to practice self-assessment is for learners to work with the assessment rubrics as they move through a course or independent learning project. For example, rubrics distinguish among levels of learning in relation to specific assessment criteria for an assignment or course, and help students incrementally judge their own work as well as to give and get feedback from their peers. Another approach to self-assessment is to have students assess their own learning during a course or independent project, where the focus is on their habits, attitudes, and aptitudes as learners. (For specific approaches and activities, see Taylor & Marienau, 2016, pp. 222–226; Taylor, Marienau, & Fiddler, 2000, pp. 63–66).

When self-assessment is driven by a learning agenda, it can be a powerful tool for bolstering adult learners' self-agency (the capacity to manage oneself) and self-efficacy (the confidence in performing well). In Kegan's framework of adult mental complexity, self-assessment can foster a "self-authoring mind" where learners set their own agendas and compass for knowing and doing (Kegan and Lahey, 2009, pp. 16, 28).

Institutional Purpose 2: Serving Adults Intentionally

Various models of serving adults intentionally have been the practice of adult degree programs for nearly 50 years (Maehl, 1999). Recently, higher education has noticed shifting demographics across all regions of the country as the proportion of the population associated with college entry has been shrinking, leading states and institutions to expand their attention to adults as a potential pool of new admissions. Additional pressures are coming from the states and federal government for greater completion rates and more adults in the workforce with postsecondary credentials. Degree completion and upgrading workforce talent have become key agenda items for many foundations. Higher education is increasingly turning its attention to the post-traditional population and the kinds of programs and services that support the success of diverse learners. This population calls for a different relationship with the institution, influenced in large measure by the distinctions and efficacies that stem from adults' rich experiences. While some may be novices in the higher education context, most adult learners are capable, often experts, in their workplaces. Prior learning assessment is a vivid example of a key practice targeted to adult students because it responds directly to the rich knowledge and competencies they bring from the workplace, the military, and other extra-institutional experiences. PLA is certainly one important practice that institutions can offer. There are also other practices for serving adults intentionally that have gained momentum as institutions have learned what powerful partners adult learners can be in the teaching–learning process.

The section that follows examines ways that admissions practices, embedded PLA strategies, and customized pathways enable institutions to serve adults intentionally and how they depend on the strategic use of assessment to do so.

Practice 1 for Serving Adults Intentionally: Admissions Assessment

Determining who gets admitted to college and on what basis is a persistent challenge for higher education. Some higher education institutions have dropped or reduced emphasis on grade point averages and standardized test scores in favor of more qualitative measures, such as personal videos, interviews, or artifacts. With respect to admission for adult and other post-traditional learners, criteria and measures that allow the individual to present her or himself in the best possible light are typically features of good practice. For adults returning to college, a low GPA from 20 years ago is not the best indicator of their current abilities, which include additional knowledge and skills that can be transferred to the institutional setting. Their score on a multiple-choice standardized test may not reflect their abilities to frame and solve problems in complex situations such as life and work.

If the goal of the institution is to produce liberally educated persons who can function well at work and contribute to their families and communities, and if the institution is truly intentional about serving adults, admissions assessments need to be congruent with this aim. Guided by Standard V (access and equity to support success), an overarching admission question might be: "How can our admission criteria and processes accommodate diverse individuals in an environment that is conducive to their learning, growth, and development?" This question suggests that admissions is a mutual decision between the institution and the individual and underscores a desired partnership between learner and institution. This question makes room for individuals to present evidence of their cognitive as well as affective and conative abilities (feeling and doing, respectively)—all of which are necessary for succeeding in a higher learning context. Cognitive abilities focus on thought and rationality; affective abilities attend to values, motivation, and appreciation; conative (behavioral) abilities enable effective interpersonal relationships and self-management interact and integrate to lead to effectiveness. Each of these three distinctive abilities requires distinctive assessment strategies. Quantitative assessment measures of cognitive abilities, while one indicator, provide an incomplete story about an individual's potential fit with an institution. Interviews with admissions staff or faculty, learning autobiographies, and work/life artifacts offer a richer story upon which to base decisions. Adults also appreciate placement "tests" that allow them to show their actual writing or numerical skills so they can be placed in courses or other offerings at the appropriate level. Some programs emphasize choice; given the outcomes of their placement exams, individuals can choose which path to follow.

Practice 2 for Serving Adults Intentionally: Embedded PLA

Despite the great numbers of adult students in higher education, many still think of themselves as outsiders in college because too many institutions are not well prepared to welcome adult learners and serve them. Adult students are quick to notice when offices are not open beyond typical business hours, when the college website and catalog use language and examples germane only to traditional learners, and when both advising and academic experiences undervalue the role of work in the lives of students. Mitigating the sense of marginalization is essential to student retention and success; prior learning assessment can be instrumental in this process. Some adult learners actively seek out opportunities for PLA. Some do not even know PLA is an option; others do not see their life experience as college material. Some institutions actively promote PLA, while many others bury it in the college catalog.

PLA, in some form, should be part and parcel of an institution's offerings, from pre-admission through graduation. But that is not enough. To serve adults intentionally, PLA options and processes should be fully visible to prospective and current students. This kind of embeddedness and visibility of PLA represents a shared purpose between the institution and the student: a partnership that strengthens the adult student's connection to the institution. The mere provision of PLA communicates the institution's basic commitment to adults. The experience of participating in PLA, particularly with portfolio, can lead learners to understand and appreciate the reasons that they are "doing college" at this point in their lives. The portfolio narrative provides context highlighting the opportunities and obstacles the learner had to navigate to accomplish what he or she did so assessors can better interpret the evidence of learning included in the portfolio. In the process of providing that contextual information, students also come to better understand the significance of their prior learning, both to higher education and to the workplace. When the institution provides support to students assembling PLA portfolios, it communicates its regard for the validity of prior learning outside of the academy and for the value-added learning outcomes of portfolio development.

Practice 3 for Serving Adults Intentionally: Customized Pathways

Ideally, assessment is a key ingredient in the processes of admission and early offerings so that each adult learner gains a clear picture of their pathway through the program. Learner-centered programs are assessment centered; they take into account the life and career goals of individual students, along with their educational goals. Rather than a one-size-fits-all approach, adult learners are able to consider options and alternative paths that best suit their circumstances, abilities, and aspirations.

We know from developmental theory that adults grow more different from one another as they mature, and their experiences become more wide-ranging (Chickering, 1981). Assessment can help ferret out *who* the learner is and how he or she learns most effectively. We also know that giving adults room to make choices on their own behalf heightens their engagement with, ownership of, and investment in their learning journey (Merriam & Bierema, 2014). Assessment generates data about the learner that he or she can actually use to make sound choices and decisions about pursuing learning that is meaningful and can transfer to work and other life contexts.

Institutional Purpose 3: The Relevant Transfer of Learning from Education to Life

Quality assurance in assessment often focuses on equitable practice within the institution, ensured by using the same assessment criteria, learning outcomes, or competencies to guide the award of credit—whatever the source of the learning. In PLA, comparability between the learning students acquire from work or other life experience with the learning students achieve within the classroom is a core measure of integrity of the PLA process (Brewer & Marienau, 2016). It is clear that assuring the consistent use of academic standards is critical, both for the sake of the institution's integrity and for equity across the experiences of diverse students. Increasingly, however, higher education is called to do more than assure consistent practice. As noted in Chapter 1, the accountability of higher education has been called into question in recent years, triggered by burgeoning financial aid debt and concerns that there is a disconnect between the requirements of higher education and the demands of life beyond it.

The growth of competency-based education (CBE) over the past 20 years or so has been fueled by this concern. A focus on demonstrable skills and knowledge, often in "authentic" assessments, is designed to narrow the gap between where learning occurs and where it is ultimately applied. Because authentic assessments are designed to provide a context and a need for students to apply their learning to solve a problem or achieve an outcome, the usefulness of learning in real life is clear. Many of the higher-profile CBE programs are also characterized by flexible delivery systems, permitting students to progress at their own pace and, in some cases, offering technology-enabled learning experiences at a lower price than more traditional programs organized according to the credit hour and time spent in learning activities. These institutions have attempted to transform the structure and content of their programs to decouple learning from time spent and from instruction delivered by the institution.

In focusing more on the outcomes of learning experiences as the indicators of learning rather than completion of particular learning experiences, CBE programs change the way colleges meet their obligation to assure quality in higher education. Conventional indicators of quality often put a high value on consistency in both the design and delivery of academic programs, leading institutions to articulate academic policy and develop programs that ensure that students' experiences will be comparable. Greater provisions for flexibility that are often central to CBE programs challenge those metrics. When different students can satisfy the same academic requirement through significantly different pathways, flexibility may be perceived, rightly or not, as sloppiness. Perhaps consistency might reside in assessment methods and standards to ensure that learning outcomes have been met rather than through practices that guide students to learn.

Must institutions adopt a CBE approach in order to ensure that their programs are relevant to life beyond higher education? Few would argue the value of a meaningful connection between higher education and the workplace, though many would argue that the needs of the workplace provide a sufficient referent for judging the quality of a college education. The demands of citizenship, community, family, and global issues also provide important measures that higher education may use both to guide the development and the evaluation of its programs. There are a variety of assessment strategies and methods that determine and enable student readiness to transfer their learning to other settings.

The following section explores how the use of authentic assessments, the cultivation and reliance on workplace partnerships, and the development and use of competency frameworks lay the foundation for assessment to tighten the link between learning and the demands of work and other life responsibilities.

Practice 1 for Supporting the Relevant Transfer of Learning: Authentic Assessments

The emergence of "authentic" assessment as a strategy for assessing student learning is related conceptually to the emphasis on "backward design" as an approach to curriculum development. Backward design (Wiggins & McTighe, 2005) emphasizes the importance of identifying and clarifying the desired outcomes of learning before designing instruction, or determining the focus of assessment as the foundation for developing learning experiences. Authentic assessment tools and practices ask learners to apply knowledge and skills to problem-solving, analysis, or creative efforts in contexts beyond higher education. For example, to demonstrate their ability to use math skills, learners might be asked to design a closet organizer; to demonstrate writing and rhetoric, they might be expected to write a letter to a legislator or to an agency to advocate for change on a particular issue. The element that authentic assessment tools have in common is the requirement that students bring learning to bear on realistic problems outside of an educational setting. While the transfer of learning to work is often the aim, faculty focus on a variety of settings closely linked to the nature of the discipline that may include family, civic, philanthropic, and recreational contexts as well.

Practice 2 for Supporting the Relevant Transfer of Learning: Workplace Partnerships

Higher education and the workplace share an interest in the competence of adults, the effective application of skills, and knowledge in relevant settings. Employers need workers who can contribute to their goals and products, and higher education needs confirmation of its responsiveness to the workplace and beyond as expressed through the success of its students and graduates.

A partnership between colleges and organizations beyond higher education can capitalize on this shared interest in a number of ways that meet the needs of both. To shrink the distance between college and work, employers might offer use of facilities and equipment for learning experiences and assessment, perhaps drawing on collaboration between subject matter experts from the workplace and educators from academic institutions who have particular expertise in assessment. Higher education is also in a position to assess and credit competencies that students acquire in the workplace and apply to their academic programs. Students can accomplish this on a case-by-case basis as they create portfolios or complete other assessments administered by faculty.

Collaboration between the college and the employer can streamline that process through the use of crosswalks that map formal employer-based training to academic requirements. Crosswalks are the result of systematic assessment of the training program and materials by faculty subject matter experts who translate the employer's formal training into PLA credit based upon evidence that the training included an assessment of the employee's skill and knowledge. The creation of crosswalks depends on a shared investment in PLA by the college and the employer and resources dedicated by both to examine the content and assessment tools used in the training being examined.

Beyond crosswalks, colleges and employers can partner to support assessment, and adult student success, by providing the college's services at the workplace. Conducting admissions interviews, pre-PLA screening, and portfolio development support at the workplace can encourage both matriculation to the college and the student's participation in PLA. The visible collaboration of the college and the workplace can provide an important support to employees who are questioning their "fit" for college.

Practice 3 for Supporting the Relevant Transfer of Learning: Competency Frameworks

A variety of competency frameworks developed outside of higher education might contribute directly to the relevance of academic programs and to the assessment of student learning. For example, the Common Employability Skills framework developed by the Business Roundtable and its national network of industry associations includes a collection of 25 competencies considered essential to success in the workplace. These include basic skills (verbal and quantitative), general disciplinary knowledge (science and technology), and noncognitive skills (interpersonal, communication and self-management). Similarly, the Connecting Credentials Framework, currently in the validation process, offers a set of competencies and various levels for each to provide a means of "comparing the levels and types of knowledge and skills that underlie degrees, certificates, industry certifications, licenses, apprenticeships, badges, and other credentials" (Lumina, 2014, p. 1). The framework makes visible the skills and knowledge shared by higher education and other organizations and offers pathways for assessing and developing them in either setting.

Institutional Purpose 4: Ensuring Consistent Practice Across Institutions

With the increased mobility of students in higher education, transferability of credit is an issue of great concern and a key part of many efforts that focus on increasing completion rates. Obstacles to credit transfer range from differing transcription styles and policies to fundamental disagreements about what kind of learning is credit-worthy. Many educational systems, both at the state and consortium level, are working toward agreement on some of the issues that compromise the transfer of credit, including credit earned through PLA rather than through course-taking. The section that follows demonstrates how assessment policy, consortia of institutions and/or organizations, and the reliance on shared resources among institutions may strengthen consistent practice across an educational system.

Practice 1 to Ensure Consistent Practice: Assessment Policy

The development and dissemination of formal policy that focuses on assessment provides an important basis for ensuring consistent practice and can serve this purpose at the institutional, state, or system level. As a collection of institutional requirements regarding assessment tools, standards, and procedures, policy documents can minimize case-by-case decision-making and advance a culture of assessment through the policy development process (See Chapter 3). Institutional policies will determine eligibility for different kinds of assessment, limits on the amount and application of credit earned in different ways, and standards associated with particular assessment tools (e.g., cutoff scores). At the state or institutional level, policies can be constructed to articulate the language and format used to transcript different types of learning and can identify articulation agreements or other assessments that apply across institutions (e.g., crosswalks, standardized tests, and related scores). Both smooth the way for students transferring across institutions and encourage collaboration of the institutions beyond policy to share approaches to training and professional development and ways to support students' engagement in assessment.

Practice 2 for Ensuring Consistent Practice: Consortia

Influenced by the national mandate from Complete College America and other forces, consortia arrangements can help create efficiency in resources and consistency in quality. Collaboration among institutions and/or organizations to evaluate nonacademic credentials and training and arrive at agreements about related credit decisions ensures consistent practice across institutions, particularly in PLA. In addition to sharing the responsibility and investment in the process, consortia clearly express standards for quality and strengthen the acceptance of credit decisions. The Consortium for the Assessment of Continuing Education (CACE) provides an example of collaboration among institutions to ensure quality in this type of assessment by working together to develop and use a single set of standards across consortium institutions (Singer, 2016).

Practice 3 for Ensuring Consistent Practice: Shared Resources

Particularly within PLA, institutions have an opportunity to increase consistent practice and stretch valuable resources at the same time. An increasing number of institutions have discovered that joining forces to create assessment tools (e.g., challenge exams and rubrics), student support (e.g., online portfolio development courses) and training opportunities (e.g., advisor, faculty assessor training) enables them to provide services they could not support individually. Further, institutions within a state or system may choose to create a single pool of assessors to broaden their reach across disciplines without increasing their institutional investment. For example, systems that have adopted LearningCounts, CAEL's online portfolio development and assessment service, often have chosen to bring CAEL in to train a pool of faculty assessors from within system institutions to be deployed by LearningCounts. Portfolios submitted by students within the system are assessed by faculty within the same system to create a shared perspective about portfolio assessment.

Other Considerations for Practice

Linking types of practices with educational purposes may provide a useful step for practitioners in the process of moving from theory to practice in assessment; for many, it might be more satisfying to review examples from specific institutions, programs, individuals, or resources. The multitude of communities of practice in higher education, adult learning, and assessment have much to offer that cannot be fairly or adequately represented here. We urge readers to investigate resources, including those provided by CAEL, to identify models, professional development experiences, and research to support their work in assessment and to become active members of those communities.

References

Adelman, C., Ewell, P., Gaston, P., & Schneider, C. G. (2014). *The degree qualifications profile*. Indianapolis, IN: Lumina Foundation. Retrieved from https://www.luminafoundation.org/files/resources/dqp.pdf

Brewer, P., & Marienau, C. (2016). The theory and practice of prior learning assessment. In V. C. X. Wang (Ed.), *Theory and practice of adult and higher education* (pp. 399–421). Charlotte, NC: Information Age Publishing.

Chickering, A. W., & Associates. (1981). *The modern American college*. San Francisco, CA: Jossey-Bass.

Fook, C. Y., & Sidhu, G. K. (2010). Authentic assessment and pedagogical strategies in higher education. *Journal of Social Sciences, 6*(2), 153–161.

Kegan, Robert, and Lahey, Lisa Laskow. (2009). *Immunity to change: how to overcome it and unlock potential in yourself and your organization*. Boston, MA: Harvard Business Press.

Lumina Foundation. (2015). *Connecting credentials: A beta credentials framework*. Indianapolis, IN: Author. Retrieved from https://www.luminafoundation.org/files/resources/connecting-credentials.pdf

Maehl, W. (1999). *Lifelong learning at its best: Innovative practices in adult credit programs*. San Francisco, CA: Jossey-Bass.

Marienau, C. (1999). Self-assessment at work: Outcomes of adult learners' reflections on practice. *Adult Education Quarterly, 49*(3), 135–146.

Merriam, S., and Bierema, L. (2014). *Adult learning: Linking theory and practice.* San Francisco, CA: Jossey-Bass.

Newmann, F. M., Secada, W. G., & Wehlage, G. G. (1995). *A guide to authentic instruction and assessment: Vision, standards and scoring.* Madison, WI: Wisconsin Center for Education Research, University of Wisconsin-Madison.

Singer, M. P. (2016). The Consortium for the Assessment of College Equivalency: Its origins and its goals. *The Journal of Continuing Higher Education, 64*(1), 56–60.

Taylor, K., & Marienau, C. (2016). *Facilitating learning with the adult brain in mind: A conceptual and practice guide.* San Francisco, CA: Jossey-Bass.

Taylor, K., Marienau, C., & Fiddler, M. (2000). *Developing adult learners: Strategies for teachers and trainers.* San Francisco, CA: Jossey-Bass.

Wiggins, G. P., & McTighe, J. (2005). *Understanding by design* (2nd ed.). Alexandria, VA: Association for Supervision & Curriculum Development.

Younger, D. (2015). Meaningful rigor in portfolio assessment. *The Journal of Continuing and Higher Education, (63)*2, 126–129.

5 GUIDING LEARNING AND DEVELOPMENT IN ASSESSMENT:
A COMMITMENT TO THE EVOLVING EXPERTISE OF INDIVIDUALS AND INSTITUTIONS

An important and often understated truth about assessment is that it is complex; the complexities become more apparent as understanding of assessment deepens. The convergence of complex variables—academic requirements, learner characteristics, institutional purposes, quality standards—inevitably makes the assessment of learning rich and complex as well as a challenging arena for practice. The implementation, maintenance, and evolution of an approach to assessing learning that generates meaningful data for all stakeholders requires a process that is intentional, inclusive, and patient. It requires institutional investment beyond the operation of assessment and development of its tools; it requires a commitment to the evolving expertise of individuals and institutions.

In Chapter 1, we highlighted the ways that changes within higher education and the social context generally warrant a new treatment of quality assurance in assessment. We expect that rapid change in education will continue, and the various changes will continue to prompt questions about how assessment is conducted and how its quality can be assured within new structures and new regulations. The evolving expertise in assessment that is essential to the health and vitality of higher education institutions relies on the engagement of individuals in the reasoning that determines the approach as well as in the delivery of services.

If institutions are to be vital and self-renewing, they need to create conditions that encourage continuous engagement with the questions that guide a thoughtful and meaningful approach to assessing learning and that capture the insights of both practitioners and thought leaders. What are the characteristics of institutions that work this way?

We have learned from other fields that learning organizations create a climate that values continuous learning through several disciplines described by Peter Senge (1990) in *The Fifth Discipline*: systems thinking, personal mastery, mental models, building shared vision, and team learning. All require intentionality, both individually and collectively, in thinking about work and applying metacognition to confirm or adjust direction toward goals or solutions to problems. Beyond subject matter expertise, practitioners gain and refine the ability to reflect and notice patterns and assumptions in their thinking that enables them to better direct it. Whether working individually or with others, these reflective practitioners (Schon, 1984) use their experience as the raw material for developing expertise that characterizes maturity within their field. Educators know students' skills in metacognition emerge across time, so they structure learning experiences to help them do so. Reflective practice is a strategy for serving the institution's purpose in developing individuals, whether practitioner or student. Learning organizations provide prompts and opportunities for reflecting about work; higher education may do the same for assessment practitioners to cultivate greater levels of expertise. While advancing the role and nature of assessment within an institution, leaders and practitioners can rely on a maturity framework, such as the Dreyfus model, to guide their reflection about practice that can lead to deepening expertise.

The Dreyfus Model for Skill Acquisition provides a matrix that characterizes increasing levels of expertise that can be applied to a variety of skill areas (Dreyfus & Dreyfus, 1980). The model was developed to describe the movement of individuals from novice to expert. We think that it may be used as the basis for describing institutional growth in similar ways. Since its introduction in 1980, the model has been used to describe the movement of individuals from simple, lower levels of ability at the outset of learning all the way to expertise characterized by rich, internalized understandings that permit agility in performance. In this model, expertise is a function of concepts derived inductively from practice and collaboration with others. It has been used by educators and trainers in a variety of settings to design learning experiences explicitly focused on cultivating expertise through experience.

Opportunities to apply the skill of reflection help the individual to discover the conditions that lead to successful practice and to develop a commitment to "doing it well" because of the value of the skills rather than the value of external validation. The premise of the model mirrors our expectations of learning processes we expect from student portfolios as adults explain how years of experience in sales, for example, have led them to not only learn common principles but to adapt some of their own.

What might this process look like for organizations? Capturing the experience of an organization is obviously much more complex than tracking that of an individual, but just as necessary. The collective experience of an organization contributes to a culture that emerges over time, reflects assumptions about its purpose, and greatly influences the way that decisions are made. Institutions working to improve assessment practices can benefit from an awareness of past experiences and use them to inform future ones. Reflecting on past efforts that were disappointing isolates them from current practice and diminishes the chance that old emotions or assumptions will influence real-time decisions and plans. Remembering past successes with similar projects can identify elements that led to success and that can be applied in the here and now.

As noted above, while the Dreyfus model has been used to describe change within individuals, we believe its tenets also hold for describing change within organizations. It has been adapted in the version that follows to propose characteristics of emerging maturity and expertise in organizations in their practices of PLA. Like novices, institutions that are new to an educational practice, such as PLA, rely on understanding rules received from an external source and, with no experience base, can do no more. With increasing experience, they develop a more complex understanding of the rules in the context of actual experience and their own emotional connection to it as a function of encountering real learners, faculty, and staff in the process of engaging with PLA. They begin to discern the elements of situations that are most relevant to effective decision-making and more quickly evaluate alternative courses of action. A strengthening commitment to refining the practice of PLA emerges with the experience of successes and failures. The institution reflects its expertise resulting from experience when it develops internalized standards and values regarding PLA that permit agility in dealing with a broad range of situations and opportunities.

We offer an example of the way the various stages appear with respect to the practice of prior learning assessment. As with applications of the Dreyfus model describing the path of individuals, the model that follows may inform the kinds of support, professional development, and structure that can help institutions progress toward expertise in PLA. If increased practice serves as the basis for developing expertise, perhaps institutions need mechanisms, both internal and external, for reflecting on their experiences and noticing patterns, aberrations, and questions that inform practice.

TABLE 3.

Stage	General Characteristics	Characteristics within PLA	Example from Practice: PLA Policy
Novice	Complies with rules Seeks affirmation of compliance from an external source Seeks accountability only to the rules	Focuses on understanding CAEL's requirements for compliance with the 10 Standards for Assessing Learning Relies on the confirmation of "success" by an authority (e.g., accrediting body) that rules have been followed	Uses CAEL's template for PLA policy including recommended language for each element of policy

(Continued)

Stage	General Characteristics	Characteristics within PLA	Example from Practice: PLA Policy
Beginner	Complies with rules Sees relationship between rules and situational factors Makes decisions driven by rules	Recognizes connections between the 10 Standards and elements of the institution's policy Utilizes faculty as SMEs Supports students through a portfolio development course	Uses CAEL's template for PLA policy and includes references to the college's offices, policies, and documents
Competent	Develops organizing principles to identify key elements in situations to guide decision-making Shifts from compliance to active decision-making and the beginning of emotional investment	Recognizes need for applying standards in ways more specifically related to the institution's programs and populations Quickly identifies consistencies and inconsistencies across circumstances that warrant explicit decision-making in order to maintain quality	Further develops policy document to represent specific circumstances, methods or tools. For example, the original statement of student eligibility is expanded to clarify the impact of incompletes, probation, etc.
Proficient	Relies more on intuition in diagnosis Makes distinct conscious decisions informed by the rules Increases risk-taking resulting from increased practice	Organizes principles drawn from a rich experience base leading to quick assessment of the way PLA can apply to emerging programs and opportunities	Uses policy document for general reference and does not amend to accommodate specific cases, though policy is used to evaluate emerging programs and opportunities as they relate to quality in PLA
Expert	Forms more intuitive decisions based on experience Uses rules to guide analysis when intuition fails	Incorporates commitment to quality in PLA while attending to other programmatic and administrative issues of the institution	Quickly determines if proposed practices, during discussions with employer partners for example, are within the boundaries of the institution's policy and acceptable practice

The chart briefly describes the different stages on the continuum from novice to expert. A look at the way a single problem or situation is addressed by institutions at different stages may help tease out the levels of maturity. Imagine that a community college has received a grant that requires that part of the funds be devoted to improving the institution's work with PLA. As the college considers avenues to pursue that will be supported by grant funds, the stages emerge.

A **Novice** institution looks to an external source, such as CAEL, for guidance. Perhaps because of misunderstandings about what is meant by PLA and inconsistent knowledge across the institution about its current PLA policy and practice, it approaches the task with no point of view about PLA and how it can support institutional goals. Decisions about grant activities are heavily influenced by recommendations from others and by what approaches other grant recipients have employed.

An **Advanced Beginner** institution recognizes past and existing practices in PLA, whether systematic or ad hoc, and frames provisional understandings of the possibilities of PLA for the institution. However, it has not had sufficient experience to have a clear perspective about what practices need revision or what new practices need to be explored. This institution often knows just enough to recognize that it doesn't know much, certainly not enough to develop a program. It elects to use grant funds to provide fundamental "Introduction to PLA" training across the institution.

A **Competent** institution has had significant experience with PLA and has engaged in improvement efforts in the past. It is aware of sources of internal support and resistance for advancing PLA and is interested in building on past successes. Practitioners have seen how PLA has made a difference for adult students and have some examples to share with others who are new to it. They plan to use grant funds or internal investments to enhance their portfolio assessment services by developing a portfolio development course. They have begun to identify alternative structures for their course by researching the field and form a task force to carry out the plan.

A **Proficient** institution has had extensive experience with PLA and is confident about the way its practices reflect quality standards. There is considerable pressure from the community and the state to articulate noncredit courses for credit and institutional leaders have seen examples of bad practice in this area by institutions that match the course designs, but don't assure that learning has been assessed in noncredit courses. They are clear that this practice is inconsistent with CAEL Standard I and decide to use grant funds or internal investments to formally examine noncredit courses in two programs and demonstrate to the institution the appropriate way to determine if noncredit courses can be eligible for credit.

An **Expert** institution has had deep experience with PLA and has rich opportunities for students to participate in PLA. Over the years, it has developed some strong partnerships with employers and has been able to create crosswalks with some to enable employees to receive academic credit for employer training. Though it is frequently approached by companies to provide the same service for them, leaders are clear that most companies in their area don't have sufficient information about their own training to start the work on a crosswalk. The institution decides to use grant funds or to seek employer funds to create a guide to evaluating workplace partners for PLA based on insights they have gained from experience over the years.

Institutions with greater "PLA Maturity" have developed a clear point of view about PLA that is based on their experience and that is refined through the lens of the institution's nature. Our Expert institution described above might exist, for example, near or within an industrial park with many needs and opportunities for partnership. Other expert institutions may not have developed a perspective about crosswalks because their community is largely agrarian, for example. They have not had experience with crosswalks because that feature was not relevant to the institution. Instead, their experience has led to expertise in PLA that focuses on ways to use technology-based assessment, given the distribution of their population.

Institutional maturity proceeds along the lines of experience consistent with the nature of the institution. Expert institutions recognize that their expertise in PLA is not evenly distributed across PLA methods, issues, or policies, but use their areas of deep expertise to evaluate their interest and readiness for experience in others.

What are the implications for an institution recognizing its position on the continuum? The Dreyfus model was and is used to plan curriculum and services to support the learning and growth of individuals. This adaptation of the model may be used to suggest professional development or other learning experiences to stimulate organizational growth. In general, professional development should be designed to support the institution in making sense of its experience with PLA and determining how it lays the foundation for improved practice. Rather than devote time and resources only to the operation and evaluation of PLA, institutions committed to evolving expertise ensure opportunities to examine assumptions and values that underlie the operation and how those may have shifted over time.

The continuum from novice to expert is characterized by a shift in the institution's investment in good practice. At earlier stages the focus is primarily on compliance, but with increased experience, institutions—and individuals—develop a more personal and immediate drive for improvement. With deepening expertise and expanding interest in improving assessment practice, institutions are poised to invest in change efforts at all levels of assessment practice. Including opportunities for individual reflection, collective self-assessment, and visioning, the institution provides opportunities to stimulate movement from one level of expertise to the next. With ongoing experience, practitioners develop the habit of regular reflection, either "real time" (reflection in action) or after the fact (reflection on action). In the next chapter, we offer the final Commitment, which focuses on taking action to achieve excellence.

References

Dreyfus, S. E., & Dreyfus, H. L. (1980, February). *A five-stage model of the mental activities involved in directed skill acquisition.* Washington, DC: Operations Research Center, University of California-Berkeley. Retrieved from http://oai.dtic.mil/oai/oai?verb=getRecord&metadataPrefix=html&identifier=ADA084551

Schon, D. (1984). *The reflective practitioner: How professionals think in action.* New York, NY: Basic Books.

Senge, P. M. (1990). *The fifth discipline: The art and practice of the learning organization.* New York, NY: Currency/Doubleday.

6 TOOLS AND RESOURCES TO SUPPORT PLA IMPLEMENTATION: A COMMITMENT TO TAKING ACTION TO UTILIZE ASSESSMENT EXPERTISE

The importance of institutional context has echoed throughout the preceding examination of quality standards, institutional commitments, and assessment practices. Context provides the touchstone for giving meaning to the purposes of assessment and the conditions in which assessment practices are designed and delivered. Context provides the community in which expertise is developed as experience is transformed into internalized understanding. This transformation occurs as the institution, at any level of institutional maturity, demonstrates a commitment to taking action that accompanies excellence in ways consistent with its mission and values.

Introducing alternative or innovative assessment practices draws on the institution's awareness of its general approach to assessment so it can enhance or expand its assessment practices. Given the growing interest and activity in PLA, this chapter offers tools that an institution may use to support its efforts in developing PLA programs that work within the context of its mission, population, organizational structure, and resources. Effective PLA programs depend on institutions carefully considering their current and historical approaches to assessment in order to choose the scale, scope, and methods of assessing students' prior learning.

- The **Institutional Readiness Guide** provides a structure for examining key elements of the institution to determine its capacity for efficiently implementing prior learning assessment. It calls for institutions to systematically gather information and perspectives to examine each of the institutional elements linked to the strategic positioning of a PLA program.

- **Forming a PLA Leadership Group** prompts institutions to consider the composition of a cross-institutional group to deliberate and guide development of the PLA program.

- The **PLA Policy Template** offers a basic structure for articulating the institution's decisions regarding essential components of a PLA program. It includes brief descriptions of the specific elements as well as sample policies related to each.

- **Portfolio Development Models** highlights optional structures for supporting students' full engagement in portfolio assessment so that institutions may choose an approach that is effective and sustainable.

These tools clearly do not address all of the elements of PLA program design and development. Instead, they are intended to launch an institution's effort regarding PLA and to model the deliberate and comprehensive consideration of PLA as a core component of an institution's academic commitment. The community of PLA practitioners can also serve as an ongoing resource for supporting the development of programs and individuals.

Institutional Readiness Guide: Positioning Prior Learning Assessment

Institution _____

Prepared by _____ Date _____

Please gather information and perspectives to examine each of the institutional elements that follow to create a picture of your institution's readiness for PLA.

1. Approach to Serving Adult Students

   Factors to consider:

   Are there specific institutional goals or initiatives directed toward adult learners?

   Is there currently a portal and/or services designed explicitly for adults (e.g., orientation)?

   Are there specific outreach strategies and/or enrollment goals for adult students?

   Have resources (human, space, or fiscal) been allocated specifically to adult student services and/or curriculum?

   Resources to consult:

2. Student Interest or Readiness

   Factors to consider:

   Have adult (or traditional) students requested opportunities to earn credit by demonstrating work/life experience-based learning?

   Are there partnerships with employers or organizations that consistently refer adults to the institution?

   Resources to consult:

3. Curriculum

Factors to consider:

Are there existing core or generic syllabi for courses that include learning outcomes written and approved by department faculty?

Have faculty provided ad hoc assessment of life-experience-based learning in order to accommodate requests by specific students?

Are there assessment practices in place at the program and/or institutional level to examine student learning outcomes (e.g., general education outcomes)?

Resources to consult:

4. Target Programs

Factors to consider:

What academic programs have existing partnerships with employers, labor unions, or professional associations?

What academic programs have existing enrollment and/or completion goals?

Resources to consult:

5. Culture

   Factors to consider:

   Over the past five years or so, what evidence has there been of the institution's interest in innovation?

   In general, what is the institution's reaction to change, either pro-active or reactive?

   What metrics does the institution regularly use to monitor its effectiveness (e.g., enrollments, completion, retention, budget, etc.)?

   Resources to consult:

6. Policies

   Factors to consider:

   Review your existing PLA policy document, or.......

   Review PLA policies embedded in general academic policy.

   How well do existing policies, procedures, and structures enable the use of workplace certifications? Standardized tests? Portfolio assessment? Evaluation of noncollegiate training or instruction?

   Resources to consult:

Institutional Readiness Summary

Use the scales below to reflect the readiness of each of the institutional elements with respect to prior learning assessment by circling the appropriate X. Below each, briefly state next steps that might be taken to move the institution forward in that area.

	Early Stages	Progressing	Ready
Approach to Serving Adults	X	X	X
Student Interest/Readiness	X	X	X
Curriculum	X	X	X
Target Programs	X	X	X

Culture	X	X	X

Policies	X	X	X

Forming a PLA Leadership Group

This **Institutional Readiness Guide** generates a good portrait of the institution's characteristics that provide a foundation for implementing or expanding PLA. The next step involves drafting an action plan to refine the components of the PLA program; set priorities for implementation; and decide who, when, and how the institution's vision for PLA will become reality.

Forming a PLA Leadership Group

Since PLA should become a well-integrated part of an institution's approach to serving adults, there is no formula for its scope, size, complexity, cost, or structure. The planning process will involve many specific choices that have impact across the institution. Forming a planning group that represents all stakeholders is the next step after assessing the institution's context.

The questions offered in Chapter 3 to guide an exploration of the quality Standards will be most beneficial to the institution when considered by a leadership group that shares a commitment to quality assessment, and that embodies a diversity of perspectives and roles.

The following list suggests various roles that might be appropriate for a PLA Planning and Leadership Team.

Academic VP or Asst. VP   _____

VP of Student Affairs   _____

VP/Asst VP, Continuing Education _____

Registrar   _____

Advisor for Adult Students   _____

Faculty/Chair (Career Programs) _____

Other Faculty   _____

Testing Center Director   _____

Assessment Director   _____

Student Representative(s)   _____

Initial Steps for the Leadership Group

If the leadership group is to create an action plan that is well suited to the institution, it must engage in some key activities first. Depending on the institution's current practice of PLA, the nature and sequence of the steps may vary, but the following components of a planning process are important to include.

Step 1: Determine the Nature of the Group

There is value in first recognizing the experiences and perspectives that group members bring to the planning process. A review of the quality Standards, guided by some or all of the questions presented in Chapter 3, will elicit the variety of assumptions and beliefs that underlie the recommendations of members. While these issues would certainly surface during the planning process, an initial review may identify likely areas of agreement and disagreement and make the planning process more efficient and meaningful.

Step 2: Develop an Institutional Approach or Philosophy for PLA

Institutions approach PLA in various ways often depending on the type of institution, its previous experiences with PLA or alternative assessment, and the influence of external organizations or agencies. The leadership group should be clear about the institution's goals for PLA and its expectations for the PLA program. Some questions it might consider:

- How does the institution regard adult learners and its commitment to them?
- What motivates the institution's interest in PLA?
- What indicators will the institution use to determine the impact of PLA on students? On the institution? On the community?
- What is the relationship between PLA and other major goals and initiatives that the institution has already adopted?

Answers to these questions will help the group plan and implement a PLA program that has the scope, components, and complexity that align with the institution's goals.

Step 3: Create or Review Institutional PLA Policy

Many institutions invest in a planning process for PLA because they seek a more systematic, equitable, and efficient process. Such a plan depends on a clear set of policies regarding PLA that are in harmony with the institution's overall academic policy. The leadership group should be thoroughly familiar with the components of an effective PLA policy document (see PLA Policy Template on p. 86) and the existing institutional PLA policy if one has been developed. Before proceeding to action planning, the leadership group should draft a PLA policy or make revisions and additions to the existing document so that the action plan will support it.

Planning the Action Planning Process

The results of the three initial steps just discussed should inform the following steps that will lead to a viable action plan. The planning process may be conducted by the leadership group or might require the involvement of additional institutional staff, perhaps organized into working groups. If the answers to questions in Step 2 above have identified specific programs that will be the early adopters of PLA, this information will influence the planning process and its players. If the policy review in Step 3 has identified key policy issues that need more inclusive deliberation, that process may require greater effort before action planning begins in earnest. Armed with clarity about the institution's purposes for PLA and existing policies that will inform it, the leadership group will be able to determine the shape of the action plan and the process for creating it.

PLA Policy template

A Guide for Institutions

Purpose of Policy

NOTE: This section is generic and intended to be used by all institutions

To recognize college-level learning students acquire outside of formal higher education, [name of college/university] relies on the following policy to ensure practices consistent with academic integrity and responsive to post-traditional learners. Such learning may be derived from various life and work experiences and the term *prior learning assessment* refers to all of the processes the college/university uses to review and evaluate evidence of learning and to award academic credit as indicated by academic and administrative standards. Adherence to this policy is also intended to support transparent transfer of prior learning assessment credit among institutions of higher education.

Policy and Procedures

Although our economy needs the experience and contributions of mature workers, people aged 55....

NOTE: This section provides a structure for institutional policy using the headings provided. Notes following each heading describe the intent of that section. Institutions should insert existing policy that applies or use institutional governance to deliberate and write policy for each heading.

Eligibility. *Policy indicates eligibility based on academic standing and/or enrollment. EXAMPLE: "Students who have earned a minimum of 6 credit hours and are currently in good academic standing are eligible to participate in prior learning assessment."*

Number of Credits. *Policy indicates the maximum number of credits a student may earn through prior learning assessment. A recommended standard calls for policy to limit PLA credits* consistent with the residency requirement or degree plan and with the guidelines of the regional accrediting agency. EXAMPLE: "Students may earn up to 50% of their degree plan through prior learning assessment as long as the residence requirement is satisfied. Credits earned through prior learning assessment are not considered part of the residency requirement."

Validation Methods. *Policy indicates the basis for evaluating prior learning. Most institutions use course equivalencies or competence equivalencies in competence-based curricula. EXAMPLE: "Prior learning must be equivalent to existing courses using the course description and course outcomes for guidance."*

This section should also list the various methods for presenting prior learning to the college/university. EXAMPLE: "The following guidelines and methods are acceptable for validating prior learning for awarding credit:"

Suggested Methods: Institutions should list all that currently apply.

1. *Credit recommendations listed in the American Council on Education (ACE) National Guide to College Credit for Workforce Training, the ACE Military Guide, and the credit recommendations of the National College Credit Recommendation Service of the New York State Board of Regents.*

2. *Credit demonstrated by successfully passing national for-credit examination programs, such as DSST Exams, Excelsior College (UExcel) Examinations, the College Board College Level Examination Program (CLEP), and Advanced Placement (AP) exams. The scores that constitute a passing score are available [in the catalog/at the Testing Center/on the website, etc.].*

3. *Degree-relevant prior learning credit awarded and transcripted by other accredited institutions.*

4. *Individual portfolios using Council for Adult and Experiential Learning (CAEL) guidelines.*

5. *Individual portfolios evaluated by CAEL's national online prior learning assessment service LearningCounts.org.*

6. *Institutionally prepared examinations. NOTE: Institutional validation procedures should be objective to the extent that external evaluators would reach the same conclusion given the material reviewed, consistent with CAEL guidelines.*

Application. *This section indicates how credits awarded from prior learning assessment will be applied to credential requirements. The following are recommended standards for applying such credit:*

1. *Prior learning credits shall be applied to meeting degree or program requirements in the same manner as credits earned at the awarding institution.*

2. *Institutions may award credit for prior learning only in those courses or program areas for which they are able to obtain a qualified faculty expert from their own or another institution.*

3. *Institutions shall award their own course title and number to the credit awarded. Neutral grades of Pass or Fail shall be utilized. Conventional letter grades shall not be used.*

Transferability. *NOTE: In the state policy guidelines, this section is used to indicate transferability among institutions. Given #3 under "Validation," there may be no need for this section in institutional policies until there is a state policy addressing transferability among state institutions.*

Fees. *This section indicates specific fees related to the entire process of prior learning assessment. This may include fees for specific tests, fees for submitting portfolios and having them reviewed by faculty for academic credit, fees for portfolio development workshops or courses. CAEL Standards should be used to determine fees and to clarify that fees are for assessment services rather than assessment results. EXAMPLE: "Students will pay an assessment fee of $250 to submit a portfolio for formal assessment. This fee is not dependent on the results of the assessment."*

Portfolio Preparation Support. *This section indicates the institution's requirements or recommendations for a student's participation in workshops, credit courses, or tutorials to support their preparation of a portfolio. EXAMPLE: "Students who choose to submit a portfolio must attend a one-hour orientation session to review basics of portfolio construction prior to submitting a portfolio for review. A portfolio preparation workshop or course is recommended for students seeking additional assistance."*

Appeals. *This section presents the process students may use to appeal a credit recommendation decision by a faculty assessor. EXAMPLE: "Students who wish to appeal a credit decision resulting from portfolio assessment may request a review of the (1) assessor's rationale for the decision and (2) the process s/he used to arrive at that decision. The PLA Coordinator will conduct the review upon formal request by the student. Students may not revise or amend the original portfolio to appeal the credit recommendation. Students who wish to revise and resubmit their portfolio for a second evaluation must follow guidelines provided in the Portfolio Development Workshop. Students may not appeal the results of standardized exams or challenge exams."*

Staff Professional Development. *This section indicates the institution's standard for initial and ongoing professional development for faculty and staff providing prior learning assessment services. EXAMPLE: "All faculty serving as portfolio assessors must complete a training that conforms to CAEL standards prior to their service as assessors. Periodic professional development will be provided by CAEL to ensure consistent practice among assessors."*

Tracking and Reporting. *This section indicates the institution's plan for tracking and reporting student participation in prior learning assessment and the results of prior learning assessment in terms of credit awarded and fees assessed. EXAMPLE: "College/University will prepare an annual report reflecting the level of student participation in each form of prior learning assessment and the resulting credit awards and costs in each category."*

Review. *"This policy shall be reviewed on a biannual basis and revised to reflect conformity with institutional academic and administrative standards."*

Effective Date: Recommended date for policy approval:

_____

Portfolio Development Models

The portfolio assessment method of PLA poses challenges for adult students, just as it often does for the institutions seeking to serve them. The portfolio provides an opportunity for learners to express their learning and competence and "make their case" that they have demonstrated course learning outcomes or other academic criteria. While the institution may offer a structure and format for portfolios, students create the substance and often need assistance in understanding the characteristics of effective portfolios. Institutions rely on a variety of structures to provide this support to students and "proactively provide guidance and support for learners' full engagement in the assessment process" (see Standard VI, p. 27). Following are key considerations for offering portfolio support in ways that are sustainable and consistent with academic integrity.

1. **Sustainability.** Is portfolio support being offered in a way that will permit growth as greater numbers of students participate in portfolio assessment?

2. **Quality.** Is there a clear distinction between supporting students' efforts and ensuring the award of credit? Portfolio development support staff should not attempt to predict the assessment of the portfolio by a subject-matter expert.

3. **Feasibility.** Does the plan for portfolio development integrate into existing structures and staffing models? Is it consistent with other forms of academic support in terms of resource allocation?

Key Decision Points in Choosing a Portfolio Development Model

Credit or Noncredit Course

Typically, this model is based on a credit-bearing course offering a full range of adult learning theory, educational planning, and portfolio development activities, such as:

Educational skill building

College orientation

Educational and career goal setting

Degree planning

Learning style survey

Structured portfolio development

Credit-bearing portfolio development courses might be designed as a blended model with weekend or evening classroom sessions followed by online assignments. Texts such as *Earn College Credit for What You Know* (Colvin, 2012) can provide a valuable planning tool to ensure that any structure the institution chooses will include key content to support the success of students with portfolio assessment.

Online, Face-to-Face, or Hybrid

Usually designed as a noncredit, structured educational activity done with a group of students. Sometimes this model combines with a freshman orientation workshop or might be offered in a work setting.

Workshop (Fee based or Free)

Small group, facilitated instruction/discussion offered at times and locations convenient for students. These typically offer less content time than a credit or noncredit course.

One-on-One Advising or Coaching

Mentoring models provide one-on-one consultation, generally with a faculty or staff member. Effective practice depends on ensuring that advising or coaching regarding portfolio development does not evolve into independent study of course material.

Self-Directed Workshops or Resources

Self-directed online portfolio workshops are noncredit bearing and may offer structured exercises, videos, workbooks, etc., to guide someone through the portfolio development process. Many online programs, like CAEL's LearningCounts.org, often include a counselor/advisor available through e-mail or phone services.

References

Colvin, J. (2006). *Earn college credit for what you know*. Chicago, IL: Council for Adult & Experiential Learning.

MISCONCEPTIONS, POOR PRACTICES, AND ISSUES[1]

Establishing an assessment program entails a series of decisions. At any juncture, misconceptions, poor practices, and unresolved issues can challenge the system. Careful deliberation and consistent monitoring of assessment concepts and practices will enhance development and continuation of effective assessment programs. Lack of attention to values, assumptions, new information, standards, or theories of learning can actually lead to termination of existing programs or disapproval of requests for resources or new proposals.

The purpose of this chapter is to highlight serious misconceptions that can lead to poor practices and to expose common poor practices. This chapter also raises some key issues that must be addressed in order to implement a successful program.

Misconceptions

1. Credit for prior learning is mainly a marketing tool to bolster adult enrollment.

Professionally responsible assessment of experiential learning certainly facilitates access and encourages enrollment. It is also true that older students, who are more likely to have

---

[1] Chapter 7 is from the 2d Ed of *Assessing Learning* (2006) and is included here with minor revisions.

more creditable experiential learning than younger ones, seek recognition and credit for their experiential learning and thus avoid redundant learning. But these reasons are not enough to attract adult learners if the educational programs are not adult friendly in other ways as well, such as including curricula responsive to adult needs and interests, teaching that is responsive to the ways in which adults are likely to learn most effectively, and administrative services that are respectful of adults' busy lives. Credit for prior learning is likely to enhance adult enrollment when it is part of an adult-oriented system.

2. Portfolio-based documentation processes, while still suspect in some quarters, are preferable to other forms of evidence for the assessment of learning gained through experience.

Portfolios, and other forms of documentation, have many attractive features. Portfolios bring together disparate strands of "learning data" to be reflected upon and compiled into direct and indirect evidence of learning for measurement and evaluation. In addition, preparing the portfolio and undergoing evaluation early in a program provides students with a clearer sense of remaining degree requirements.[2]

However, it is a misconception to judge one form of documentation as better than another. The best forms of documentation make the learning assessable. The realization of this principle, then, rests on the clarity of the expected learning outcomes and the criteria to be applied to measure the level of learning. These factors set the context for deciding what appropriate forms of evidence may look like, from examinations to performance in simulations, to testimonies or observations of applied learning in live contexts, to portfolios.

---

[2] For a discussion of portfolios and various strategies for their use, see Elana Michelson, Alan Mandell, and contributors, *Portfolio Development and the Assessment of Prior Learning: Perspectives, Models, and Practices*, copyright 2004, Stylus Publishing.

3. It is improper to offer both credit and pay for experiential learning that takes place on the job.

This misconception often accompanies the discussion of internships, cooperative education assignments, and other work-and-learn programs. The source of this misunderstanding is the common confusion between experiential activities and learning outcomes. In fact, payment or compensation is primarily given for the activity, while credit is awarded for the outcome. The experiential activity for which the employer pays is an input; the learning gained from the experience(s) for which credit or other credentialing may be awarded is an outcome.

The evaluation of learning and the award of credit are processes separate from the acquisition of learning, just as they are in a classroom. In experiential learning, it doesn't make sense to differentiate between the learning of volunteers and the learning of paid workers if a valid assessment indicates that they have learned the same thing, unless the learning objectives involve something about the nature of volunteering itself.

4. Only courses taken on campus should be accepted for residence credit.

A policy requiring a fixed proportion of credits to be earned in residence is based on two assumptions: first, that campus-based courses always have some added value as they are taken within a community of scholars and, second, that learning acquired elsewhere does not provide this advantage. If the institution can demonstrate that learning outcomes are more aligned with its criteria for quality when the learning occurs in residence, then these assumptions are obviously validated. However, the premise that there is something special to be gained from immersion in a community of scholars is difficult to defend on commuter campuses. Many working students rush onto campus just before class and depart immediately afterward. If it is the presumption of quality assurance for teacher-directed education that underscores the residency requirement, unless the same assurance holds for the assessment of the learning outcomes, this comes close to equating input with the defining element of a quality residence-based education. The rapid infusion of distance-based education programs of many kinds—from degree granting to certificate offering to credentialing programs—is perhaps the ultimate challenge to defining the meaning of residence and its importance to policy formation.

Besides, it isn't necessarily accurate to conclude that the experiential learner was totally denied the advantages of a community of scholars. With the highly mobile community of contemporary life, scholars are found in the workplace, at dinner parties, in the family, and in the media (including on the Internet). It is certainly the case that the structure and organization of the learning can differ significantly when it occurs on a college campus and that there is more opportunity for informal participation in a community of scholars in a resident situation. However, without describing the advantage of a residency in terms of the learning outcomes, it is quite difficult to justify the residency requirement. Where learning takes place and how it takes place are not necessarily equivalent. Residency requirements may become less prevalent as experience-based learning is developed as the intended objective of education.

5. Credit for experiential learning should not be granted at the graduate level.

Opposition or resistance to granting graduate-level credit to learning from experience comes in several forms: concern for quality assurance, the belief that graduate learning is somehow so different that it cannot be attained anywhere except in graduate school or post baccalaureate credentialing programs, and concern over decreased enrollment if the practice were to become widespread.

Actually, each of these sources of opposition is frequently belied by the actual practices of most graduate schools. While there may be resistance to the idea of granting credit for external learning, it is already going on under a different name in the form of waivers, substitutions, and alternate methods of satisfying requirements. Each of these practices takes into account prior learning. What results is a respect for not requiring repetitive learning, which is handled as a change in the requirements, not a reduction of them.

A graduate degree under these conceptions can be considered value-added in contrast to a chronicle of competence.

As with so many other misconceptions about the role assessment can play in the design of education, if graduate, as well as undergraduate degrees, were defined in terms of learning outputs—demonstrable competence in specified knowledge and skills—the overemphasis on inputs might be diminished and the meaning of a degree would align more closely with a conception of generally acceptable evidence of specified levels and amounts of learning.

6. Awarding advanced placement without credit and waiving requirements are reasonable alternatives to awarding credit for prior experiential learning.

This concern is related to the previous misconception. It is more common in undergraduate education, however, to waive requirements without credit and replace them with the expectation of additional course work. For example, students with demonstrable competence in a foreign language may be placed in advanced classes but denied credit for their competence. This practice results in a value-added but distorted meaning of a baccalaureate degree. The student with the equivalent learning of, say, six credit units still must make up those six units by taking additional electives. The student ends up over-fulfilling the requirements, reaching the same level of competence that is required of all students in the foreign language area and completing six more credit units than other students. Again, the misconception underlying this practice is that a degree depends on the amount of time spent rather than on the learning outcomes achieved.

Poor Practices

1. Granting credit for experience, not learning.

Grievous enough to be considered malpractice, this activity is the essence of Standard I and the persistent theme throughout this book. It is highlighted here because the practice still exists. The granting of credit or a credential on the basis of time served, rather than on learning outcomes achieved, is a major violation of good assessment practices.

2. Basing assessment fees on the number of credits awarded.

This is a direct violation of Standard VIII. When credits are awarded for fees, two serious negative results occur: it inaccurately reflects the true costs of assessment, and it injects a profit motive into a decision that should be made only on academic grounds. The real cost of assessment may be the same for a "no credit" decision as for a more positive finding. It makes sense to set fees in terms of units assessed but not in terms of units awarded.

The negative influence of a profit motivation can be either personal or institutional. It is probably most important for for-profit institutions to pay particular attention to this; although, not-for-profit institutions can be just as prone to place revenue above good practices. On the individual side, this practice can be a problem when the assessor's compensation is dependent on the number of units granted.

The only way to ensure quality in the award of academic or credentialing credit is to ensure that the charges for assessment are, in fact, based on the cost of assessment and not the award of credit.

3. Promising that credit is likely to be awarded.

Even in institutions and programs where substantial care is taken to grant credit for learning, not experience, a careless approach to advertising often implies that a credit award is likely. Once a prospective student's expectations have been raised by catchy World Wide Web ads or brochures with statements such as "Your life experience can earn college credit," assessors may find themselves on the defensive and have a difficult time enforcing the standards.

It is not an easy process to prepare a portfolio or evidence of learning. Good practice requires that materials on learning assessment state the following facts: credit is only granted for learning; an applicant for credit is expected to invest significant time and effort in making the case that experience has, in fact, resulted in creditable learning; it is not possible to know in advance whether (or, if so, how much) credit may be awarded; and the final determination of credit or credentialing awards will be based on expert measurement and evaluation of that learning.

4. Judging learning from experience too early in the assessment process is likely to negate the deserved award of credit or a credential.

When an advisor or mentor prematurely judges the prospects for a credit award, the process of assessing learning is compromised as a complete review of evidence of learning is deemed unnecessary. This activity is the flipside of the poor practice of implicitly promising credit for simply describing experience. The identification step should be a patient exploration of the possibilities. It is certainly realistic to expect an experienced advisor to anticipate that some claims to learning by a student may indeed never see the awarding of credit or a credential. However, students who are new to the process of PLA often first need time and space to surface and describe significant events in their lives before they can articulate their learning at a level of detail and depth that will ultimately be required for documentation and evaluation. Inhibiting the mining of the possibilities by prematurely derailing the process may hinder the surfacing of a student's tacit knowledge. It is also likely to inhibit students from trying again, at a future date, to bring forth creditable learning, even though it may very well be present.

5. Involving incompetent persons in assessment and evaluation.

Standard IV states that the persons responsible for assessing and evaluating the learning must have relevant expertise in the subject matter content, as well as in the assessment process. These two types of expertise are required for determining levels of competence and awarding credit. It is certainly possible to find individuals who embody both kinds of expertise. Full-time, regularly appointed faculty decidedly should possess both content and process expertise in their areas of specialization. Experiential learning, however, crosses boundaries of both disciplines and place, and requires individualized assessment. A single faculty member may be qualified in part of the content and in part of the appropriate assessment procedure, but not necessarily in all of both. More than one assessor may be needed for a sound assessment. Further, a qualified assessor might not be a member of the full-time faculty but someone who, by virtue of her/his applied knowledge and relevant context, can determine the academic or professional meaning of a student's learning and in the value of a particular competence. Institutions may be tempted to save money, time, or effort by relying on insufficiently prepared assessors or by limiting assessment to certain areas of knowledge that reside in the faculty, rather than including experts from the wider community.

Once the assessment process is underway, incompetent assessment is sometimes the result of misguided, though sincere, attempts to be objective, such as seeking to avoid contact between the assessor and the learner. While the virtues of anonymity are gained, the advantages of probing through personal contact are lost. The assessment deficiency that results may be in either direction: the award of credit that is not deserved or the failure to uncover, and give appropriate credit for, learning that the isolated petitioner did not her/himself recognize or report in the proper manner.

As assessment processes become institutionalized, approaches (e.g., portfolio) can become mechanized; specific measurable parts supersede the gestalt, or the details overshadow important generic capabilities. Credentialing by regulatory authorities or institutions with expanding and large enrollment is probably most susceptible to these pitfalls of making routine a process that, by its very nature, has strong elements of individualization.

6. Granting credit for progress rather than for attaining learning that meets the agreed upon criteria.

This activity is a common practice in some academic cultures. It is possible, of course, for someone to expend considerable effort and make a great deal of progress, but still not achieve a level of competence that is appropriate for the credit or credential. What makes this troublesome practice difficult to eliminate is that effort and progress are thoroughly commendable learning objectives. It is difficult to argue against a vision of education in which all individuals learn all that is possible and appropriate for them to learn, while taking into account where they started and how far they are capable of going. What amounts to a poor assessment practice, however, is to confuse effort and progress with that of achievement of creditable levels of competence. Summative evaluations (i.e., grades) lose meaning or credibility if grading or other summative judgments are based on progress and not on achievement, unless the criteria for doing so are agreed upon and public.

7. Restricting the assessment of experiential learning for credit to only certain areas of a curriculum without a clear rationale.

It is common for programs to allow credit by assessment of prior learning in some areas of the curriculum and not others. Some programs do not allow credit for experiential learning in a major but do allow it in general education areas or vice versa. It is the prerogative, of course, of any program or institution to insist on participation in the community of scholars that constitute the faculty in a particular segment of offerings. Residency requirements raise the question of whether the learning outcomes do, in fact, differ for in-residence learners and for experientially-based learners. Without a clear rationale for their policies, programs and institutions often send a mixed message regarding their commitment to criteria-based assessment.

Anticipated Issues

When establishing a sound assessment program with well-prepared assessors, numerous issues will arise, many of which may be anticipated. Assessment entails a series of decisions guided by standards and principles and open to interpretations based on mission, values, philosophies of learning or education, and degrees of knowledge about assessment and evaluation processes. Predictably, issues lurking below the surface of an institution or organization often come to the surface during assessment.

We've selected four issues for which, like any good issue, there are multiple perspectives that form sides from which to derive a resolution, at least until there is sufficient unrest to revisit the issue again. The standards and principles can help frame the arguments that the issues can generate although they don't offer codified solutions.

1. How is individual learning recognized within collaborative learning contexts?

There is little argument that contemporary work and community life demands collaborative and cooperative capabilities. The collective achievement of goals inevitably leads to a degree of shared knowledge and learning that may not reside solely in one individual. Academic achievement, however, is often viewed as an individual accomplishment based on the belief that each person is accountable for what she/he has learned. Without even challenging this tenet, an assessment question emerges of no small proportion: How does one fairly and appropriately assess a person's competency when it has been developed with others and to meet goals not connected explicitly to the academic enterprise?

2. Who is excluded by assessment policies and practices?

The concept of variation and individual differences in learning preferences and strategies is widely accepted and respected in the areas of teaching and learning. With regard to assessment, however, attention to individual differences hasn't reached the same level of consideration. Physical limitations, preferences for expression of knowledge in media other than text, the extent to which emotional intelligence is converted to affective knowing, and a host of other ways to describe and analyze learning outcomes expand or limit the scope of the assessment capabilities of any program or individual assessor. Consequently, policies that assume some forms of assessment are more appropriate—not necessarily more valid—than others inherently exclude some portion of most populations. How responsive to individual differences should assessment policies and practices be?

3. What financial model best supports an assessment program: self-sustaining or subsidized?

The ultimate goal of most institutions would be to establish an assessment program that holds itself accountable, generates resources for improvements and growth, and is self-sustaining so that it is not susceptible to a reduction of resources or changes in administration. Another incentive for a self-sustaining model is that assessment can be built into faculty load. Over the long run, expecting faculty to carry out the tasks of assessment without reducing their course load can erode an assessment program that is successful in all other ways.

The expenses of a quality assessment program include salaries and honoraria, space, professional development, and materials, along with shared costs such as physical plant and administrative services (e.g., transcription). A key step on the road to being self-sustaining is to segregate all the functions associated with the assessment process and determine the costs for each. Students should be responsible for the basic costs of assessment (which can be done reasonably, especially when they do not pay for assessment by the credit [see Standard VIII].) The principal assumption here is that the cost of assessment alone should be less than the cost of assessment when it is linked to instruction, which is the norm in classroom-based education.

Since assessment is rarely viewed as a central function of an educational institution, decisions about financing assessment efforts can translate into important, but differing, strategic outcomes—short- and long-term. It doesn't take a detailed analysis to draw a correlation between the complexity of assessment measures and the costs incurred by their development, implementation, and associated quality-assurance measures. Following is an illustration of the spectrum of assessment measures that could—and probably should—form the inventory of a well-developed assessment program:

- Performance simulation
- Interview/dialog (w/assessor)
- Tangible product (e.g., work based)
- Testimony from qualified observers
- Subject-based essay
- Standardized exam (e.g., CLEP, "local" challenge exam)
- Self-assessment

None of these is necessarily used alone, and several are often combined in practice. Yet often a majority of programs limit both their repertoires and their invitations to measure students' learning to the middle of the group: essays, standardized exams, and work products. And though there is not a recent survey of the measures education providers draw on, it is likely that associated costs are as much as, or more, a factor in this decision as is assessment philosophy. What financial models should be applied to the establishment, maintenance, and expansion of the capacity of a quality assessment program?

4. How does online learning change the face of assessment?

In most aspects, the standards and related principles should provide sufficient touchstones for assessment efforts, whether the relationships between institution and students are campus based or mediated by electronic media, such as the Internet (e.g., World Wide Web, e-mail). At this point in the evolution of digitized, distant relationships, there are two major issues regarding online assessment programs.

The first issue concerns the range and means of evidencing learning that is available for students. Even more than campus-based programs, online assessment privileges text; that is, it tends to limit students to visual representations of what they know. Incorporating aural (auditory) and kinesthetic modalities for online assessment is a challenge of the future.[3] Also, the anonymity that is tempting but not ideal in campus-based relationships is more likely to be the norm in online programs.

The second issue concerns authenticity of students' work. How do we know for sure that the work submitted was actually created by the student? Assessment interactions, in large measure, rely on good faith and at least a basic level of trust in the honesty of all parties. Do the same presuppositions hold true for online assessment as for campus-based, or does online, by its very nature, require a re-evaluation of them?

---

[3] Since 2006, notable advancements have been made in online learning; auditory and kinesthetic modalities are now commonplace. For example, online simulations are used in business schools, nursing programs, and medical schools.

The emergence of technology to both store and retrieve information and documents, as well as mediate communications, is bringing with it opportunities to lower some of the costs of assessments and increase efficiencies, as well as access for all parties involved. Some interactions currently done face-to-face may be replaced by asynchronous communications at a distance; in turn, experience with asynchronous communications may highlight those exchanges that really are better carried out by direct, person-to-person interactions with skilled personnel.

In Conclusion

Misconceptions, poor practices, and issues that lead to unanticipated decision-making can impede the development of sound assessment programs that respect and promote learning from experience. But they can also endanger the quality of assessment and evaluation in traditional programs as well.

Adherence to the 10 Standards and the principles and procedures of Chapters 4, 5, and 6 can go a long way toward helping organizations, colleges, and universities meet acceptable, if not high, standards of quality. At the very least, the conversation that ensues can lead to a variety of desirable outcomes, from heightened awareness of the criteria for quality assessment to the application of good assessment practices for individual and organizational improvement.

A

STEPS AND PRINCIPLES FOR ASSESSING UNSPONSORED PRIOR EXPERIENTIAL LEARNING

Step 1. IDENTIFICATION: Review experience to identify learning that is potentially creditable or appropriate for credentialing

- 1.1 Develop strategies for describing learning experiences
- 1.2 Differentiate between learning and experience
- 1.3 Specify learning outcomes
    - 1.31 Allow sufficient time and patience to arrive at specific learning outcomes
- 1.4 Use assessment to promote and reinforce learning
- 1.5 Facilitate re-entry into an academic culture and future learning
    - 1.51 Provide guidance, i.e., printed materials, websites, advising and other resources
    - 1.52 Institute a formal structure for helping people to identify possible creditable learning

Step 2. ARTICULATION: Relate proposed credit to academic, personal, and professional goals

- 2.1 Determine what is creditable
- 2.2 Align the articulation with criteria for acceptable level of learning outcomes
    - 2.21 Note issues for later attention

2.3 Relate proposed creditable learning to program objectives

    2.31 Create a process to help learners articulate their learning, personal goals, and program goals

    2.32 Enhance learner self-awareness through the articulation process

2.4 Consider the recency of learning

Step 3. DOCUMENTATION: Prepare evidence to support claim for credit

3.1 Make sure assessment is based on evidence

    3.11 Formulate policies regarding the role(s) of documentation

3.2 Documentation should reference what is creditable learning

3.3 Develop perspectives and policies on primary and secondary forms of evidence and documentation

    3.31 Specify appropriate types of documentation

    3.32 Provide examples of various types of documentation

    3.33 Determine and make public the appropriate uses of documentation

    3.34 Communicate that learning is experiential

3.4 Authenticate evidence

    3.41 Create procedures for authentication of submitted evidence

    3.42 Request that documentation addresses the learning outcomes and establishes the qualifications of the individual to represent an individual's learning

    3.43 Request that secondary documentation address learning outcomes, not qualities of the learner per se

3.5 Judge quality of evidence, not quantity

3.6 Make documentation contribute to learning

Step 4. MEASUREMENT: Determine the degree and level of learning/competence achieved

4.1 Fit assessment methods to the learning

4.2 Fit assessment methods to the learner

4.3 Measure outcomes, not inputs

4.4 Utilize assessment as learning

4.41 Develop and practice assessment methods that promote further learning

4.5 Ensure reliability

4.51 Use more than one sample of evidence when possible

4.52 Use more than one assessor

4.53 Avoid various forms of bias, discrimination, or unconscious error in judging a student's work or performance

4.6 Ensure validity

4.61 Assess learning by comparing to learning objectives

4.62 Seek different forms of evidence of learning; use more than one type of assessment

4.7 Train assessors; seek training as an assessor

4.71 Written guidelines and training materials should be available and sought out by assessors

4.72 Match assessment training to assessment method

4.73 Maintain consistent conditions

4.8 State results; provide feedback

4.9 Encourage and develop self-assessment skills

4.91 Have learners participate in the design and administration of assessment process

Step 5. EVALUATION: Determine the credit equivalency

5.1 Decide who categorizes and defines competencies

5.2 Maintain integrity and equity by making criteria transparent

    5.21 Evaluate an individual's learning in relation to transparent criteria

    5.22 Employ subject matter and assessment expertise

    5.23 Relate criteria for crediting or credentialing learning to institutional goals and character

5.3 Provide a clear and rational basis for awarding credit for learning from experience

    5.31 Adopt and justify the credit model appropriate for the institution and the outcomes of learning

    5.32 Rationalize any limits to the amount of learning that can be credited

    5.33 Specify basis for translating assessed outcomes into credit hours or credentialing thresholds

    5.34 Consider accommodation of partial credits for assessed outcomes

5.4 Establish the same or comparable standards for measuring teacher-directed and experiential learning outcomes

    5.41 Specify basis for translating assessed outcomes into credit hours or credentialing thresholds

5.5 Credit or recognize learning, not experience; outcomes, not inputs

5.6 Provide useful feedback

    5.61 Establish guidelines for the quality and characteristics of good feedback

    5.62 Precede each new major learning activity with a review of prior learning

    5.63 Provide summative feedback as soon as possible following an assessment

5.64 Follow the assignment of credits for assessed learning with advice on implications for degree or credential requirements

5.65 Extend advising on the outcomes of an assessment to include plans for future learning

5.7 Consider alternative forms of recognition for assessed experiential learning

5.71 Provide options for partial credit that may also be sufficient as prerequisite credit

5.8 Provide for review and appeal

5.81 Treat review of individual assessments as part of a comprehensive program review

5.9 Avoid awarding of duplicate credit

Step 6. TRANSCRIPTION: Prepare a useful record of results

6.1 Communicate with third parties

6.11 Succinctly describe individual learning

6.12 Retain the functions of a transcript while recording learning outcomes

6.13 Establish panels for review of narrative transcripts

6.2 Set policies regarding transcripts

6.21 Provide information that validates and legitimizes assessed learning

6.3 Record learning appropriately

6.31 Find alternatives to misleading course labels

6.32 Describe learning outcomes, not experiences

Appendix

B

ADMINISTRATIVE MEASURES TO ENSURE QUALITY PRINCIPLES AND PROCEDURES

Publish Policies and Procedures

Standard VII: Assessment policies and procedures are the result of inclusive deliberation and are shared with all constituencies.

> 7.1 Articulate a rationale for assessment policies
>
> > 7.11 Support decision making with a clear rationale
>
> 7.2 Create a clear process for review and change of policies
>
> > 7.21 Create levels of review such that each level contributes to the quality of the decision making
>
> 7.3 Derive policies and practices from an integrated curriculum
>
> > 7.31 Determine what experiential learning is effective in completing curriculum requirements
> >
> > 7.32 Clarify how assessment and experiential learning function in relation to other components of the curriculum and institution/organization
> >
> > 7.33 Develop an operational model for assessment and experiential learning
>
> 7.4 Clarify roles and responsibilities

7.5 Create a centralized source (handbook) of policies, procedures, roles, and responsibilities

    7.51 Include all elements of an assessment program

    7.52 Provide the same handbook to professional personnel and students

    7.53 Ensure "truth in advertising"

7.6 Protect individual privacy

7.7 Determine perspectives and policies regarding individual differences

Develop Appropriate Fee Schedules

Standard VIII: Fees charged for assessment are based on the services performed in the process rather than the credit awarded.

8.1 Charge fees for assessment, not for credit

    8.11 Make clear what services will be provided for an assessment fee

    8.12 Make fees proportional to the amount of anticipated assessment effort

    8.13 Establish fees independent of the assessment outcome

8.2 Ensure cost-effectiveness

    8.21 Ensure equitable fees for students and pay for faculty

8.3 Recognize assessment as a contribution to learning

    8.31 Remunerate assessors on the basis of expertise and effort, not credit hours awarded

8.4 Monitor cost-effectiveness and efficiency

    8.41 Establish prices that are equitable in relation to actual cost of assessment and the real benefit of the assessment process itself

Professional Development Is a Reciprocal Responsibility

Standard IX: All practitioners involved in the assessment process pursue and receive adequate training and continuing professional development for the functions they perform.

9.1 Identify who can and should participate in the assessment process and clarify their respective roles

    9.11 Create a rationale for who is included in and excluded from an assessment process

    9.12 Establish qualifications of assessors

9.2 Determine the number of assessors who should evaluate an individual's learning

9.3 Specify responsibilities of assessors and associated personnel

    9.31 Design training to meet the responsibilities

    9.32 Expect an understanding of both the broad and technical aspects of assessment

    9.33 Use assessors who have knowledge of both their specialty and general assessment

9.4 Create a culture to ensure quality through continued learning

    9.41 Provide training and ongoing professional development to everyone connected with assessment

    9.42 Provide feedback to new assessors

    9.43 Inform assessment personnel about accreditation rules

    9.44 Set high expectations and reward performance

Evaluate Experiential Learning Programs

Standard X: Assessment programs are regularly monitored, evaluated, and revised to respond to institutional and learner needs

- 10.1 Foster professional standards
    - 10.11 Designate review personnel
    - 10.12 Study the results of reviews; identify areas for resolution of differences
    - 10.13 Involve outside reviewers
    - 10.14 Evaluate assessment methods and strategies
- 10.2 Seek agreement on practices
    - 10.21 Periodically check on levels of agreement among personnel regarding policies and practices
- 10.3 Monitor authenticity
    - 10.31 Inform students of authenticity procedures
    - 10.32 Periodically check on assessor verification of documentation and authenticity of self-reports
- 10.4 Monitor consistency of assessment
    - 10.41 Use periodic review to evaluate quality of assessment procedures
    - 10.42 Discontinue involvement of unreliable assessors and methods
- 10.5 Use appropriate technical procedures
- 10.6 Monitor value of assessment to those affected by it
    - 10.61 Select assessment methods that maximize learning and development of learners
    - 10.62 Assess value and quality of assessment from perspective of various stakeholders
- 10.7 Implement periodic program evaluations
    - 10.71 Articulate standards for measuring effectiveness of assessment program

WRITING STATEMENTS OF LEARNING OUTCOMES

Statements of learning outcomes are fundamental to a transparent assessment process. Stating learning outcomes that are assessable, however, can take practice. Here are two examples of outcome statements for someone who is to be assessed for her knowledge of psychology at an undergraduate level:

> Can write a 10-page essay explaining differences between Freud and Jung as expressed in one of the following texts: x, y, or z.
>
> Can apply at least two models of psychodynamic analysis to analyze family relationships.

A good outcome statement suggests the level of learning that is expected as well as the area of content without being too specific so that one's learning can only fit into predefined boundaries. In addition, a useful outcome statement should suggest but not prescribe possible evidence. In the absence of articulated learning outcomes for any given domain of creditable learning, the risk of an arbitrary or idiosyncratic assessment of someone's knowledge or skills is great. With good outcome statements, both assessors and individuals being assessed are converging on the same point from different directions—the assessor with a judgment on the individual's knowledge or skill leading to a decision regarding credit or credentialing and the individual with the gathering or creating of evidence of his/her learning shaped by the outcomes by which it will be evaluated.

Without the benefit of articulated outcome statements, assessors may inadvertently ask learners to demonstrate learning at a level that is above or below the standards applied to course-based students as well within a broader or narrower scope. Much flows from well-framed learning outcome statements: additional specific criteria as well as agreements between program, assessors, and students regarding expectations, possibilities, and boundaries for evidence.

The first of the two examples has several problems with it—the nature of the evidence is prescribed (in a ten-page essay), the level of performance is ambiguous (the student must demonstrate understanding), the scope is unclear (the student is asked to explain differences), and the sources of acceptable information are restricted. This statement leads at once to an assessment that is overly broad and simultaneously restrictive such that it would accommodate only a small population of people who may have delved into psychology on their own. The second example asks for a level of learning for which additional criteria may be readily available ("analysis"), a scope that is probably representative of many undergraduate curricula ("at least two models"; "family dynamics"), and an open set of possibilities as to how these outcomes may be demonstrated.

INDEX

A

Academic credits, 25, 43, 69, 86, 88
Acquisition of learning, 95
Action planning, process for, 85
Adult degree programs, 1, 50
Adult learners, 16, 49. *See also* Serving adults, models of
  assessment process, 17
  development of, 44
  feedback, 17
  self-assessment of, 28
Advanced beginner institution, 68
American Association of State Colleges and Universities (AASCU), 2
American Council on Education (ACE), 5, 8, 22, 87
Assessing Learning (1989), 6–7
Assessment fatigue, 30
Assessment of learning
  anticipated issues, 102–106
  financial model for (*See* Financial model, for learning assessment)
  formative, 23–24, 43
  goals for, 14–18
  higher education, 4
  involving incompetent persons in, 100–101
  key institutional commitments for, 6–7

limitations of, 18
online learning, 105–106
policies and practices, 103
purpose of (*See* Purpose of learning assessment)
quality assurance mechanism, 18, 54
quality standards for (*See* Quality standards, for assessing learning)
role of PLA and CBE in, 4–6
summative, 23–24
transfer from education to life, 54–58
Assessment programs, 93, 102, 105
  development of, 106
  effectiveness of, 116
  evaluation of, 31, 116
  expenses of, 104
  financial model, 103–105
  online, 105
  review and revision of, 32
Association of American Colleges and Universities (AAC&U), 2, 4, 43
Association of Public and Land-grant Universities (APLU), 2
"Authentic" assessment, of
  student learning, 56
  tools and practices, 56
Award of credit. *See* Credit awards

B

Backward design, for
  curriculum development, 56
"Bleeding red pen
  phenomenon," 48
Business Roundtable, 58

C

CAEL standards, for assessing
  learning
    evolution of, 36–38
    portfolios evaluation, 22, 60
    ten quality standards, 21–39
Clarity, concept of, 47
Classroom-based education,
  104
Coaching, 28, 46, 92
Collaborative learning, 103
College education, quality of, 55
College-employer
  collaboration, 57
College-level learning, 15, 36,
  46, 86
Common Employability Skills
  framework, 58
Competency-based education
  (CBE), 1, 2, 3, 43
    academic programs, 5
    assessment strategies within,
      5
    growth of, 54
    relation with PLA, 6
    role of, 4–6
Competency-based learning
  (CBL), 43
Competency-based Network
  (C-BEN), 4
Competency frameworks, for
  higher education, 56, 58

Competency levels,
  determination of, 25–26
Competent institution, 68
Connecting Credentials
  Framework, 58
Consortium for the Assessment
  of Continuing Education
  (CACE), 60
Continuing education units
  (CEUs), 26
Cooperative education
  assignments, 95
Corrective feedback, 48
Credit awards
  alternatives to, 97
  determination of, 25–26
    guidelines for, 25
  earned in residence, 95–96
  evaluation of learning and,
    95
  experiential learning for, 102
  judging learning from
    experience, 99–100
  for prior experiential
    learning, 97
  for progress, 101
  quality in, 98
  student's expectations, 99
Credit by exam, 22
Credit course, 89, 91
Credit, for prior learning, 94
Credit transfer, obstacles to, 58
Critical reflection, learners'
  assessment processes, 16–18
  emotional load, 17
Crosswalks, 57, 59, 69
Curriculum, development of,
  28, 29
    backward design for, 56
    Dreyfus model for, 70
Cutoff scores, 59

D

Decision-making, 106
  deliberative, 32–34
Degree Qualifications Profile
  (DQP), 4
Departmental challenge exams,
  22
Dewey's conditions for genuine
  learning, 14–15, 18
Directive feedback, 48
Disciplinary-oriented
  programs, 26
Disorienting dilemmas, concept
  of, 15–16
Distance-based education
  programs, 96
Documentation, portfolio-
  based, 94
Dreyfus Model for Skill
  Acquisition, 64–65
    general characteristics of,
      66–67
    for planning curriculum, 70

E

Educational programming,
  quality of, 28
Education programs, distance-
  based, 96
Emotional load, 17
Empathy, in learning, 47
Employee's skill and
  knowledge, assessment of, 57
Essential Learning Outcomes, 4
Excellence in Assessment (EIA),
  2, 3
Experiential learning, 100
  adult enrollment in, 93–94
  assessment of, 93
    credit for, 95, 102
    at graduate level, 96–97
    evaluation of, 116
    Kolb's theory of, 18
    pay for, 95
    unsponsored, 107–111
    value-added, 97
Expert institution, 69–70

F

Facilitative feedback, 17, 48
Feedbacks
  for adult learners, 17
  "bleeding red pen
    phenomenon," 48
  corrective, 48
  directive, 48
  facilitative, 17, 48
  forms of, 48
  qualitative, 47–48
  to students, 41
Fees
  charged for assessment,
    29–30
  schedules, 114
Financial model, for learning
  assessment, 103–105
Flexibility, in assessment of
  learning, 47
FLOOR model, of adaptive
  strategies, 7

G

Genuine learning, Dewey's
  conditions for, 14–15
Guide for institutions, for
  learning assessments, 86–90

H

Higher education, 1–2, 50,
54–57, 64
  assessment of learning in, 4
  default pattern, 17
  educational interventions, 5
  purpose of, 43
  role for assessment in, 2–4
    with PLA and CBE, 4–6
Higher education institutions
  assessment services,
    sustainability of, 29
  compensation to faculty, 29
  conflicts of interest, 30
  curriculum development, 29
  evaluation cycles, 31
  fee structure, 29
  in-house program, 29
  practice across (*See* Practice
    across institutions)
  purpose of learning
    assessment (*See* Purpose of
    learning assessment)
  revenue incentives, 30
  tuition, credit-based, 29

I

Inclusive deliberation, concept
  of, 28–29, 85, 113
Incompetent persons, in
  learning assessment, 100–101
Individual differences in
  learning, concept of, 103
Individual learning, 103
Individuals, development of,
  43–50
  formative power of
    assessment, 43
  higher education, 43

notion of, 43
  preparation and support for,
    45–47
  qualitative feedback for,
    47–48
  self-assessment for, 48–50
  self-perception and, 45
Industry certifications, 26, 58
Integrity, in assessing learning,
  47–48
Internships, 95
Interpersonal relationships, 49,
  52

K

Kolb's theory, of experiential
  learning, 18
Kuh, George, 1

L

Learners' full engagement,
  guidance and support for,
  27–28
LearningCounts.org, 22, 29,
  60, 92
Learning from experience
  assessment in relation to, 7
  assessment process, 99–100
  graduate-level credit, 96
  process of, 16
  theories of, 14, 18
Learning outcomes, criteria for,
  24–25
Liberal Education for America's
  Promise (LEAP) initiative, 4
Lindquist, Jack, 6
  FLOOR model of adaptive
    strategies, 7

M

Mezirow's theory, of transformational learning, 15, 18
Microcredentials, 26
Misconceptions, in learning practices, 93–97

N

National Institute of Learning Outcomes Assessment (NILOA), 3
National standardized exams, 22
New learning
  assessment process, 16
  commitment for, 15
  design to foster, 15–16
  disoriented dilemmas and, 15–16
  individual's experiences, impact of, 15
  Mezirow's perspectives on, 15
  perspective shifts and, 15
Noncredit course, 69, 91
Novice institution, 68

O

One-on-one advising, 92
Online learning, 105–106
Online portfolio development courses, 60

P

Perspective shifts, concept of, 15
Placement, without credit requirements, 97
Poor practices, in learning assessments, 98–102
Poor test takers, 45
Portfolio assessment services, 27, 68, 89
Practice across institutions, 58–60
  assessment policy, 59
  consortia, 59–60
  other considerations for, 60–61
  shared resources, 60
Prior learning assessment (PLA), 1, 2, 27, 35, 50, 65–66
  action planning, process for, 85
  credit for, 94
    alternatives to awarding, 97
  embedded, 52–53
  institutional policies
    creation of, 85
    purpose of, 86–90
    review of, 85
  institutions approach, 84–85
  leadership group
    determination of nature of, 84
    formation of, 83–84
    initial steps for, 84–85
  operation and evaluation of, 70
  policy templates, guide for institutions, 86–90

portfolio for, 14, 45–46, 53,
57
development models of,
90
key decision points, 91–92
procedures for, 86–90
relation with CBE, 4–6
role of, 4–6
student's participation in, 57
tools for (*See* Tools for PLA
programs)
Professional designations, 25
Professional development,
29–31, 59, 61, 66, 70, 104, 115
Proficient institution, 69
Profit motivation, influence of,
98
Purpose of learning assessment
for ensuring consistent
practice across institutions,
58–60
individuals, development of,
43–50
for serving adults
intentionally, 50–54
for transfer of learning from
education to life, 54–58

Q

Qualitative feedbacks, 47–48
Quality assurance, 96
in learning assessment, 18,
54, 63
procedures for, 28
for teacher-directed
education, 95
Quality principles and
procedures
fee schedules, 114
professional development,
115
publishing of, 113–114
Quality standards, for assessing
learning, 106
assessment programs,
evaluation of, 31
CAEL's 10 Quality
Standards, 21
competency levels,
determination of, 25–26
credit awards, determination
of, 25–26
criteria for learning
outcomes and, 24–25
decision-making,
deliberative, 32–34
for diverse individuals and
groups, 26–27
evidence of learning, 22–23
and fees charged for
assessment, 29–30
formative and summative,
23–24
institutions assessment
approaches and practices,
28–29
learners' full engagement
and, 27–28
for professional
development, 30–31
shifts in, 35–39
Quantitative assessment, of
cognitive abilities, 52

R

Residence-based education, 96
Residence credit, 95–96

S

Self-assessment, 27, 48–50, 70
Self-directed workshop, 92
Senge, Peter, 64
Serving adults, models of,
  50–54
  admissions assessment,
    51–52
  customized pathways, 53–54
  embedded PLA, 52–53
Situated learning, Lave and
  Wenger's theory of, 18
Standards for Assessing
  Learning, 6, 21, 22–31
Statements of learning
  outcomes, 117–118
Student learning, 41
  assessment of, 4
    "authentic" assessment as
      strategy for, 56
    award of credit, 26
    key institutional
      commitments for, 6–7
  movement for, 1
  PLA and CBE approaches
    for, 4–6

T

Teacher-directed education, 95
Teaching, learning, and
  assessment (TLA) centers, 31
Technology-enabled learning
  experiences, 55
Tools for PLA programs, 73–74
  action planning process, 85
  institutional policies

creation of, 85
purpose of, 86–90
review of, 85
institutional readiness guide,
  75–82
institutions approach, 84–85
leadership group
  determination of nature
    of, 84
  formation of, 83–84
  initial steps for, 84–85
Training, employer-based, 57
Transcription, 42, 58, 104, 111
Transfer of learning
  authentic assessments, 56
  competency frameworks, 58
  from education to life, 54–58
  workplace partnerships,
    56–57
Transformational learning,
  Mezirow's theory of, 15, 18
Tuition, credit-based, 29

U

Uses of assessment data, 6, 8

V

Valid Assessment of Undergraduate Education (VALUE),
  4
Variation in learning, concept
  of, 103
Voluntary System of
  Accountability (VSA), 2

W

Waiving requirement, 97
Work-and-learn programs, 95
Workplace partnerships, 56–57

Workshop
  fee based/free, 91
  self-directed, 92
Writing statements, of learning
  outcomes, 117–118

CPSIA information can be obtained
at www.ICGtesting.com
Printed in the USA
FSOW03n1557050517
33932FS